FIGHTING FIT

As an intelligence officer in the British Army between 1985 and 1991, Adrian Weale took part in operations and training with the Special Air Service, Special Boat Service, Paras, Commandos and other special forces. In *Fighting Fit* he has used this experience to show you how to achieve the high standards of physical fitness that are the hallmark of the elite units of the British Army.

ADRIAN WEALE

FIGHTING FIT

The SAS Fitness Guide

CHAPMANS

Chapmans Publishers
A division of The Orion Publishing Group Ltd
Orion House
5 Upper St Martin's Lane
London WC2H 9EA

First published by Chapmans 1993

A CIP catalogue record for this book is available from the British
Library

ISBN 1–85592–680–6

Photoset in Monophoto Plantin by
Selwood Systems, Midsomer Norton

Printed and bound in Great Britain by
Butler & Tanner Ltd, Frome and London

CONTENTS

ACKNOWLEDGEMENTS

I WOULD PARTICULARLY like to thank the following people for their help in putting together *Fighting Fit*: Caroline Mercer, who took a lot of time and trouble devising the recipes in the food chapter; Piers Hill, for the use of several of his training ideas and for his general overview on the work in progress; Simon Weale (my brother) for allowing himself to be photographed by me; Mark Crean, for his encouragement and ruthless editing; and Andrew Lownie, Tim Lupprian, Julian Mercer, Christopher Geidt, Peter Simons and Mary, my wife, who had to put up with me while I was writing the book and who mercilessly stamped on my literary pretensions. I would also like to thank the members of 21 and 22 SAS, as well as the Airborne and Commando Forces, who I cannot individually name but who gave me much advice and help.

INTRODUCTION

EVER SINCE B SQUADRON of 22 SAS blasted their way into the Iranian Embassy in London on 5 May 1980, the Special Air Service Regiment of the British Army has enjoyed a reputation as a shadowy band of highly trained supermen. One component of the SAS legend concerns the physical fitness of its members, whose strength, stamina and endurance are reputedly enough to make a grown man cry. Just ask any member of the SAS and he will reassure you – it's all true!

There are a number of very good reasons why the SAS and other elite forces prefer to maintain a low profile and why their operational techniques are kept secret. Don't look through this book for detailed instruction on silent killing because you won't find it. Instead, *Fighting Fit* shows you how to acquire the physical and mental toughness that are the hallmarks of the Special Air Service, the Paras and the Royal Marine Commandos. Neither is beyond acquisition by a physically normal but well-motivated person – after all, who else are they going to recruit?

There is no single type of SAS soldier – they come in most shapes and sizes – but what they have in common is a determination to succeed. There are two SAS selection courses every year and about 150 hopefuls turn up for each of them; by the end, 28 weeks later, there will normally be less than 30 left to join the Regiment. If you're a soldier, or you want to join one of the Territorial Army's SAS units, the Paras or the Commandos, then this book shows you how to train and prepare for their selection courses using methods that have worked successfully for a number of candidates, including some who are still serving. If you're a civilian who just wants to get fit or lose weight, *Fighting Fit* is a no-flimflam guide which will do just that as quickly and painlessly as possible. And if you're just reading this out of curiosity, then consider these facts:

---

1 In a typical year in the United Kingdom, 150,000 people will have a heart attack and 240,000 people will be diagnosed as suffering from cancer.

2 Unfit men are nearly twice as likely to suffer from heart disease and *four* times more likely to die of cancer than fit men.

To me, these are good reasons to get up and start taking exercise.

Fighting Fit makes no claims to have discovered any special techniques or tricks which will make getting fit any easier, and it is not an official publication of the SAS or any other part of the armed forces. While I have never been an operational member of the SAS, I have distilled the techniques and methods used by those who have joined the elite forces the hard way – through the front door – to produce exercise programmes and a diet guide which, when combined, will make an enormous difference to the fitness level of anyone who uses them sensibly. Additionally, there is a chapter on the Great Outdoors for those who enjoy walking in the hills, and there are training programmes that will get potential recruits to the start of several elite selection courses in peak condition. There is no need to give up alcohol, there is no requirement to count calories religiously (which most people find impossible to do anyway) and you don't have to wear skin-tight lurex clothing in public. What could be better?

How to Use This Book

Unless you are already very fit and used to taking exercise, do not attempt any of the exercises in this book until you have read and understood all of it because you may do something wrong and injure yourself. Similarly, the SAS Selection programme recommends exercise in mountainous and remote areas; it would be very foolish to attempt this without a good knowledge of navigation, survival and first-aid techniques of the sort practised by the armed forces.

The author and the publishers can accept no responsibility for any injury or illness suffered by any person attempting the activities described in this book. If you have any doubts about your ability to perform them, seek the opinion of a qualified medical practitioner.

CHAPTER 1
RAW
MATERIAL

THE BODY

TO UNDERSTAND HOW to get the best from exercise, it is a good idea to have some knowledge of how the human body is put together and how it works. This section is a quick explanation of the basic structure and operation of the musculo-skeletal system.

Muscles

Muscles are bundles of fibres which are attached to your skeleton and can be expanded and contracted to move you about. They generally operate in opposing pairs so that one controls a movement in one direction, while the other has an opposite effect. An example of this are the biceps and triceps – the biceps enables you to flex your arm and the triceps extends it. Exercise causes the muscle tissue to break down and then rebuild in a stronger form, more able to cope with the particular demands placed on it. This means that different types of exercise produce different effects. Body-builders, for instance, exercise by performing small numbers of repetitions with very heavy weights, creating large, bulky muscles, whereas endurance athletes create muscles more suitable for extended use by exercising with much lighter weights for many more repetitions.

The Skeleton

Your skeleton is the frame to which your muscles are attached, and so, to a large extent, it determines your size and shape. The size and shape of your skeleton is determined mainly by genetic inheritance and the quality of your nutrition when you were growing, but exercise and good food now will help to strengthen it.

Body Fat

The body needs to contain a certain amount of fat to maintain normal function. For men the ideal proportion is about 15 per cent, for women about 20 per cent. Less than that, and you are more likely to become vulnerable to infections; more, and fat begins to accumulate in places where it shouldn't, making you look flabby and, more importantly, interfering with your circulation and other body functions.

Body Shape

Your body shape and weight are defined mostly by your musculature, your skeleton and your body-fat ratio. You can't necessarily do anything about your skeleton, but with properly exercised muscles and your fat percentage around the ideal level, your body will work efficiently and look good. Dieting alone will help you to lose weight (in some cases), but without muscle tone you will be what body-builders call 'skinny fat'. Yuk! All of the exercises in *Fighting Fit* are designed to help you achieve the right balance.

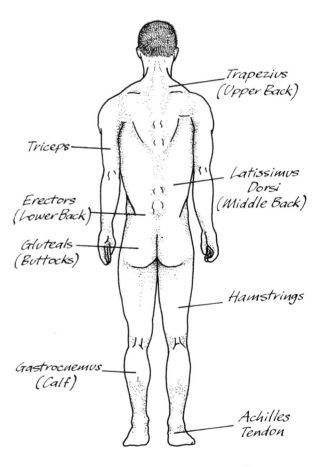

Trapezius (Upper Back)

Triceps

Latissimus Dorsi (Middle Back)

Erectors (Lower Back)

Gluteals (Buttocks)

Hamstrings

Gastrocnemus (Calf)

Achilles Tendon

THE BODY

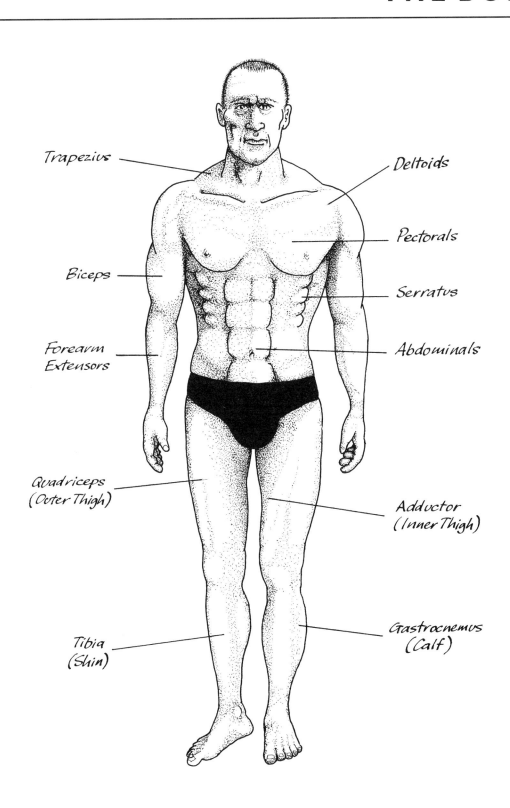

Trapezius

Deltoids

Pectorals

Biceps

Serratus

Forearm
Extensors

Abdominals

Quadriceps
(Outer Thigh)

Adductor
(Inner Thigh)

Tibia
(Shin)

Gastrocnemus
(Calf)

HEIGHT AND WEIGHT

ONCE YOU HAVE become fit, you will be carrying far less excess fat around with you. Physically, the main thing that Arnie Schwarzenegger and Madonna have in common is that their shape is defined by muscle bulk. Madonna has the muscular definition without excessive size that aerobic exercise creates, while Schwarzenegger has a body built for power. Unfortunately, the fact is that most of the rest of us are far too fat for our own good.

How do you check whether you have too much fat? Easy, get your gear off and stand naked in front of a full-length mirror. If you feel that you look fat then you probably are; alternatively, jump up and down and jog on the spot – the bits that are wobbling around on your hips and stomach are almost certainly fat. But don't be disheartened – everybody gets a bit porky from time to time, and before the jungle training and combat survival phases of SAS selection most recruits are desperately trying to gain weight and fat reserves to help stave off the stress induced by a dramatically restricted food intake!

Now weigh yourself and note the result. The height-to-weight tables on this page indicate the correct weight range for your height. Be honest with yourself when you're using them because if you are significantly outside these limits (more than about 7 lb or 3.1 kg), then it is possible that you might be taking a risk by exercising.

Do You Weigh Too Much?

If you are greatly over the weight limit for your height, the first thing to do before starting an exercise programme is to go to see your doctor and check that your body is up to it. One of the risks is that you will be imposing a fair amount of extra strain on your joints,

increasing the risk of injuring yourself. More importantly, you are increasing the workload on your heart, lungs and other vital organs – possibly to the extent of causing a heart attack. When you use the exercises in the Fighting Fit programmes in Chapter 5, substitute swimming for running, minute for minute, until you've lost enough weight to allow you to run comfortably. In addition, approach all other exercises, like gym work, with a certain degree of caution.

Do You Weigh Too Little?

If you are significantly underweight, you should also get yourself checked by a doctor before starting an exercise programme. It is possible that you will be imposing excessive stress on yourself by trying to undertake exercise without sufficient reserves to do so, and it may be that you have an eating disorder or some other illness. You will certainly need to eat more to be able to cope with the exercise in the Fighting Fit programmes.

And Anyway

Don't be complacent about your weight, as it is an important factor in your fitness and health – but don't get hung up about it, either. You may find that your weight will increase by a few pounds at the start of your exercise programme: this is caused by your body building muscle tissue, which weighs more than fat, and you will soon lose it again. If you injure yourself or become ill and are unable to train, you will almost certainly gain some weight – check out Chapter 6 for how to deal with this.

On average, a champion male marathon runner is 5 ft 10 in (1.78 m) tall and weighs 10 st (64 kg), while a good heavyweight boxer will be 6 ft 4 in (1.93 m) and 15 st (95 kg). If we are fit and eating the right foods, our bodies will find the right weight for the demands that we make on them.

It is a common myth that muscles turn to fat if you reduce or change your exercise pattern. This is actually an impossibility but there is a danger that, if you don't reduce your food intake, you won't burn off sufficient calories. This will mean that your muscles reduce in size but you gain fat. The answer is to follow Schwarzenegger's example; if you ease back on training, ease back on eating at the same time so that you reduce your muscle bulk painlessly.

HEIGHT AND WEIGHT

Desirable Weights for MEN   *Weight without Clothes – Height without Shoes*

Height Ft In	Small Frame St lb St lb	Medium Frame St lb St lb	Large Frame St lb St lb
5 4 (1.62 m)	8 6 – 9 8 (53.5–57.5 kg)	8 12 – 9 10 (56.5–62 kg)	9 6 10 8 (60–67.5 kg)
5 5 (1.65 m)	8 9 – 9 3 (55–58.5 kg)	9 1 – 9 13 (57.5–63 kg)	9 9 – 10 11 (61.5–68.5 kg)
5 6 (1.68 m)	8 12 – 9 7 (56.5–60.5 kg)	9 4 – 10 3 (59–65 kg)	9 12 – 11 2 (62.5–71 kg)
5 7 (1.70 m)	9 2 – 9 11 (58–62.5 kg)	9 8 – 10 7 (61–69 kg)	10 2 – 11 7 (64.5–73 kg)
5 8 (1.72 m)	9 6 – 10 1 (60–64 kg)	9 12 – 10 12 (62.5–69 kg)	10 7 – 11 12 (67–75.5 kg)
5 9 (1.75 m)	9 10 – 10 5 (62–66 kg)	10 2 – 11 2 (64.5–71 kg)	10 11 – 12 2 (68.5–75.5)
5 10 (1.78 m)	10 10 – 10 0 (63.5–68 kg)	10 6 – 11 6 (66.5–72.5 kg)	11 1 – 12 6 (70.5–79 kg)
5 11 (1.80 m)	10 4 – 11 0 (66.5–70 kg)	10 10 – 11 11 (68–75 kg)	11 5 – 12 11 (72.5–81.5 kg)
6 0 (1.83 m)	10 8 – 11 4 (67.5–72 kg)	11 0 – 12 2 (70–77.5 kg)	11 10 – 13 2 (74.5–83.5 kg)
6 1 (1.85 m)	10 12 – 11 8 (69–73.5 kg)	11 4 – 12 7 (72–79.5 kg)	12 0 – 13 7 (76.5–86 kg)
6 2 (1.88 m)	11 2 – 11 13 (71–76 kg)	11 8 – 12 12 (73.5–82 kg)	12 4 – 13 12 (78–88 kg)
6 3 (1.90 m)	11 6 – 12 3 (72.5–77.5 kg)	11 13 – 13 3 (76–84 kg)	12 10 – 14 3 (81–90.5 kg)
6 4 (1.93 m)	11 10 – 12 7 (74.5–79.5 kg)	12 4 – 13 8 (78–86.5 kg)	13 0 – 14 7 (82.5–91.5 kg)

I RAW MATERIAL

13

HEIGHT AND WEIGHT

Desirable Weights for WOMEN *Weight without Clothes – Height without Shoes*

Height Ft In	Small Frame St lb St lb	Medium Frame St lb St lb	Large Frame St lb St lb
5 0 (1.52 m)	6 12 – 7 6 (43.5–47 kg)	7 3 – 8 1 (46–51.5 kg)	7 11 – 8 13 (49.5–57 kg)
5 1 (1.55 m)	7 1 – 7 9 (45–48.5 kg)	7 6 – 8 4 (47–52.5 kg)	8 0 – 9 2 (51–58 kg)
5 2 (1.57 m)	7 4 – 7 12 (46.5–50 kg)	7 9 – 8 7 (48.5–54 kg)	8 3 – 9 5 (52.5–59.5 kg)
5 3 (1.60 m)	7 7 – 8 1 (47.5–56 kg)	7 12 – 8 10 (50–55.5 kg)	8 6 – 9 8 (53.5–61 kg)
5 4 (1.62 m)	7 10 – 8 4 (49–52.5 kg)	8 1 – 9 0 (51.5–57.5 kg)	8 9 – 9 12 (55–62.5 kg)
5 5 (1.65 m)	7 13 – 8 7 (50.5–54 kg)	8 4 – 9 4 (52.5–59 kg)	8 13 – 10 2 (57–64.5 kg)
5 6 (1.68 m)	8 2 – 8 11 (52–55.5 kg)	8 8 – 9 9 (54.5–61.5 kg)	9 3 – 10 6 (58.5–66.5 kg)
5 7 (1.70 m)	8 6 – 9 1 (53.5–57.5 kg)	8 12 – 9 13 (56.5–63 kg)	9 7 – 10 10 (60.5–68 kg)
5 8 (1.72 m)	8 10 – 9 5 (55.5–59.5 kg)	9 2 – 10 3 (58–63 kg)	9 11 – 11 0 (62.5–70 kg)
5 9 (1.75 m)	9 9 – 9 0 (57.5–61.5 kg)	9 6 – 10 7 (60–69 kg)	10 1 – 11 4 (68.5–72 kg)
5 10 (1.78 m)	9 4 – 10 0 (59–63.5 kg)	9 10 – 10 11 (62–68.5 kg)	10 5 – 11 9 (66–74 kg)

I RAW MATERIAL

SMOKING, DRINKING AND drug abuse are all factors which can have a serious effect on your physical fitness and general health. Smoking and boozing remain socially acceptable despite their highly unpleasant side-effects (like death), but anyone who tries to get fit while doing either – or both – is barking mad. I know; I used to smoke 30 a day!

Smoking

If you're a smoker who takes exercise, you tend to get used to the feeling of constriction in your chest, the rasping in your throat and the coughing fits when you finish. However, I can assure you that life is a whole lot more pleasant without them. All the scare stories are true, unfortunately, and the fact is that you are massively increasing your chances of an early death if you carry on smoking. I gave up after reading a book called *The Easy Way to Stop Smoking* by Allen Carr (published by Penguin Books). This put me into the correct frame of mind and, coupled with the exercise

I was taking at the time, genuinely helped a great deal. I am against the use of nicotine chewing-gum or patches because you are just substituting one addiction for another, but they do work for some people. Whatever method you use, *stop smoking!* It's not big, it's not clever and it even makes you smell.

Alcohol

Nobody minds too much if you have a few drinks every now and again, but if you are getting wrecked as a fruit bat every night then you've got problems. In fact a beer or two, taken after exercise, can help you to replace energy used up during the session and unwind psychologically. Two pints of beer contain between 400 and 500 calories, together with a slack handful of vitamins, and this is easily metabolized by your body. Most of us will have experienced the negative side of alcohol, however. This includes hangover – a combination of alcohol poisoning and dehydration which is enough to stop anyone from taking exercise; obesity – caused

> The health risks caused by smoking regularly are far greater than those for being overweight. To cause the same statistical risk to health as smoking 20 cigarettes a day, a 5 ft 8 in (1.68 m) man who normally weighs about 10 st 7 lb (67 kg) would have to weigh 15 st (95 kg).

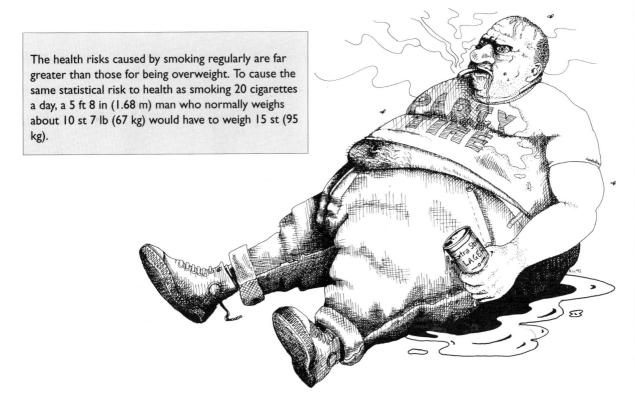

by those 200-odd calories per pint; and the stupid, dangerous things that we tend to do when under the influence. All this should be enough to tell you that alcohol is fine in moderation, but you need to be careful. It is all too easy to get into the habit of drinking a lot – and from there to alcoholism is only a small step. Analyse your drinking habits: Do you drink much when you're on your own? Do you find yourself drinking during the morning? Do you drink to overcome problems? Do you regularly get wrecked mid-week? If the answer to any of these is 'yes', then it is possible that you have a drinking problem and you need specialist help.

Drugs

I have never taken any illegal drugs in my life and I'm not about to start – the risks far outweigh the benefits. If you are addicted to, or dependent on, any type of drug you need specialist help, not an exercise handbook. Put *Fighting Fit* to one side until you've started to get to grips with your problem, then you'll be ready for it. If you're using drugs for sneaky performance benefits, read on . . .

The problem with substances which mask pain or temporarily boost performance is that they can hide the effects of serious damage. Pain is nature's way of telling you to stop the activity which causes it. If you have taken drugs which prevent you from feeling pain, it is possible that you could do serious damage to yourself without realizing it and then exacerbate the injury by continuing to exercise. The effect of using steroids and other such performance-boosters is more long-term; they will improve your performance at the potential expense of serious problems later in life. Athletes who use illegal drugs to boost their sporting performance are missing the point of what it's all about, anyway.

Finally, a word to any military personnel reading this who are now, or who might be contemplating, using illegal drugs. Don't. The effects of a machine-gunner having a bad LSD flashback, for example, don't bear thinking about. If you are addicted, declare the problem to a doctor or *padre* and you will be treated very sympathetically. If you hide it, the chances are that you will get caught by those nasty fellows with the bright red hats.

Medical Factors

Physical handicaps are no barrier to becoming extremely fit within the limitations that the handicap imposes. *Fighting Fit* contains a wide variety of exercises that can be adapted into very rewarding exercise programmes for the handicapped. Similarly, recovery from serious illness or injury is also not necessarily a barrier to becoming extremely fit and strong. There are many examples of sportsmen and women who have suffered serious injuries coming back to compete at the top level. Look at Paul Gascoigne; in 1991 his career appeared to be finished after he injured his leg in the FA Cup Final, but within two years he was back, playing a key role in the fortunes of the England soccer team.

However, there are several medical factors which should affect your attitude to starting an exercise programme. The most important among these is a history of heart or circulatory diseases, in yourself or in your family. In 1984, Jim Fixx, an American fitness guru, died of a heart attack while running his daily 10 miles. More than anyone else, Fixx was responsible for the start of the exercise boom in the USA, yet he had a history of heavy smoking, obesity and job stress over a long period. He had eliminated all of these factors from his life, but enough damage had already been done to combine with the inherited tendency towards heart disease and sentence him to death.

Other problems that might creep up and ambush you include arthritis and skeletal disorders, though they are less likely to have such a dramatic effect.

Don't Give Up!

Your medical history will only stand in your way if you let it. I'm not suggesting that you cast away your crutches and do SAS selection (though in the 1950s 'Lofty' Large came back from two years of malnutrition in a Korean POW camp with an arm virtually paralysed from a sniper's bullet to do just that), but you can still give yourself the self-confidence, inner strength and toughness that only the genuinely fit have. The current US Army recruiting slogan is 'Be All You Can Be' – good thinking. You owe it to yourself to succeed.

SO HOW FIT ARE YOU?

BEFORE YOU BEGIN any of the Fighting Fit programmes it is important to run a couple of tests on yourself so you'll know where to start.

Resting Heart Rate

The first thing is to establish your Resting Heart Rate. This is the speed at which your heart is pumping when your body is not doing anything else. The best time to do it is first thing in the morning, just after you've woken up. Remove your watch (if you're wearing one) and put it where you can see the second hand or counter. Take your left wrist in your right hand and lightly press the tips of your right index and middle fingers into the space just below your thumb. Move your fingers around until you can feel a pulsating sensation – and there you are! Once you can feel the pulse strongly, look at the watch and measure off 15 seconds while, at the same time, counting the number of beats you get from the pulse. Multiply the result by 4 and that is your resting heart rate per minute. Now compare the result with the table below:

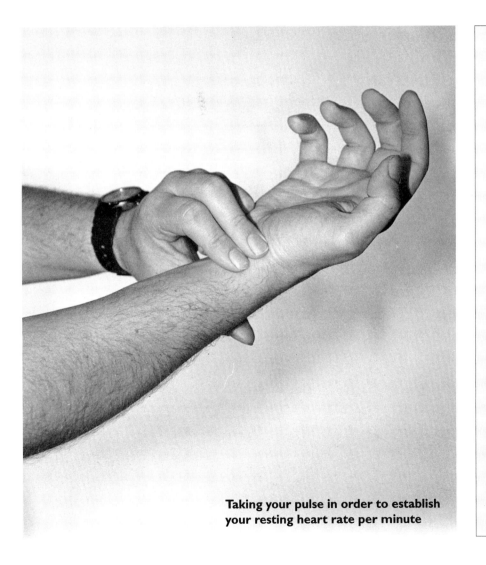

Taking your pulse in order to establish your resting heart rate per minute

Beats per minute	
100	unfit
90	
80	average
70	fit
60	
50	very fit
40	
30	

Women's hearts tend to beat slightly faster than men's. Women can give themselves 5 beats per minute leeway on these figures.

The figures go down as you get fitter because your heart pumps more blood with each beat and so needs to beat less often to do the same job.

I RAW MATERIAL

SO HOW FIT ARE YOU?

The Step Test

A far more reliable way of gauging your fitness is to measure your heart's ability to recover from exertion. The best way of doing this is to try the Step Test. Don't attempt this if you have ever suffered from heart trouble or if you have any doubts at all about your ability to perform a moderately hard workout.

First, get dressed in loose, comfortable clothing: a T-shirt, shorts and training shoes are ideal. You will also need to find yourself a watch and a step or stool 6–10 in (15–26 cm) high. When you are ready, practise a few times to get the feel of the speed of the test. All you have to do is step up on to the step like so: Left foot on, left foot off, right foot on, right foot off, twice in 5 seconds. When you are happy with your ability to do this at the correct rhythm, take a few minutes' rest.

OK, get psyched up, this is your first session on the road to Fighting Fitness. Get your watch out and start stepping! Keep going for exactly 3 minutes, then stop and rest for exactly 30 seconds. Now count your heart-beats (using the Resting Heart Rate method) for exactly 30 seconds. This will give you a number and you can compare it with the chart below:

Age	20–39	40 & Over
Men	**Number of Beats**	
Excellent	34–38	37–40
Good	37–41	40–43
Average	41–43	43–45
Acceptable	43–47	45–49
Poor	48–59	50–62
Women		
Excellent	39–42	41–44
Good	43–45	44–47
Average	45–47	46–49
Acceptable	47–53	48–55
Poor	48–59	55–66

The Step Test

It has been found that cross-country skiers and biathletes have the lowest heart rates. Cross-country skiing requires prolonged exertion of the legs, arms, back and abdomen; resting heart rates of 30 beats per minute and under are not uncommon among cross-country ski champions.

ONE OF THE GREAT JOYS of real fitness training is that it needn't cost very much money; in fact, you've probably already got most, if not all, the kit that you need. If what you have is too clapped out, and you want to stock up, this is what you will need:

Shoes

A good pair of running shoes is essential in order to prevent blisters, callouses, bunions and other more serious injuries to your feet and legs. The best shoes will keep your feet stable as you run, provide enough cushioning for even the heaviest runner and have gripping soles which will prevent you from falling on most surfaces. I have used shoes by Nike, New Balance and Hi-Tec which are all excellent, but many other makes are equally as good. The best place to buy running shoes is in a specialist running store rather than a general sports or shoe store, as the sales staff will usually know more about what they are selling.

Socks

The best sort of socks are made from loop-stitched wool/nylon mix. These feel a little like towelling and are very comfortable on the feet. You can get them just about anywhere where socks are sold.

Tops

An ideal running top should keep you warm when it's cold and cool when it's warm and not interfere with your movement at all. Unfortunately a top like this has yet to be invented, so make do with a T-shirt or vest instead and a sweatshirt for when the weather is cold. Among the SAS and Paras, Helly-Hansen 'Lifa' thermal vests have become very popular and they do stay quite warm when wet.

Shorts

At present, running shorts can be found in two distinct styles: traditional shorts or the skin-tight 'cyclist' type.

I prefer the traditional shorts because I don't much like the idea of innocent passers-by being able to count every wrinkle on my package as I jog towards them. Even so, cycling shorts do help to prevent chafing on your thighs which can be eye-wateringly painful.

Sports Bra

I'm reliably informed that sports bras make life considerably more comfortable for women taking exercise. The 'Minimal Bounce' brand is highly recommended. Who am I to argue?

Basic Extras

There are a few little extras which don't cost much but can be useful. A jar of petroleum jelly is essential to help prevent chafing, blisters on toes and 'jogger's nipple'. If you've got long hair then wear a headband to keep it out of your eyes, and sweatbands on your wrists are also useful.

Finally, if you've got enough money, consider investing in a sports Walkman. These are water-resistant, they can play while you're running and they are great for staving off boredom – whether you listen to the B-52s, Bach or a teach-yourself-Burmese tape.

> Wear and tear on sports equipment that is used regularly is often much greater than on normal clothing. Bear this in mind before you spend a lot of money on expensive kit because it may not last long. If you are serious about getting fit, your wisest investment will be on the best pair of running shoes that you can afford; grotty T-shirts, shorts and socks don't cause injuries but badly fitting or clapped-out running shoes can.

I RAW MATERIAL

CHAPTER 2
BASIC
TRAINING

ENDURANCE VERSUS POWER

THE EXERCISES DESCRIBED in *Fighting Fit* fall into two groups. Cardio-vascular exercises – the first group – build endurance by making your heart, lungs and circulation more efficient and adaptable. The second group, power exercises, build strength in individual muscles and muscle groups. This chapter describes the exercises that form the Fighting Fit programmes; Chapters 3 and 5 show you how to put them together to build a comprehensive package.

Aerobic and Anaerobic

You build up endurance by using aerobic cardio-vascular exercises. Aerobic means 'with air' – you exercise using the air you are taking in through your lungs. 'Anaerobic' exercises, on the other hand, like sprinting, only use the small amount of oxygen that is stored in your muscles. Typical aerobic exercises include running, swimming, cycling, walking, rowing and cross-country skiing; the sort of 'aerobics' practised at sports centres and gyms has only a nodding acquaintance with fitness training, though undoubtedly it makes you feel better.

The aim of aerobic exercises is to raise your heart rate into the training range where the 'overload principle' comes into effect. In English, this means that you have to raise your heart rate to the level indicated in the table below. If you can maintain your heart at that rate for about 30 minutes, your body will 'realize' that your heart has been overloaded and it will compensate by building extra muscle in the heart and improving your circulatory system to allow you to do it again. The next time you take that form of exercise, you should find it marginally easier, because your body will have adapted towards being able to do it. If you don't take any further exercise, your body will, fairly quickly, lose its adaptation and return to normal.

Concentrating only on cardio-vascular exercise would probably leave you thin and very wiry; in other words, fit and healthy but not in a position to take on the rigours of SAS selection or P-Company where you have to carry heavy weights about.

Power Training

The missing ingredient is power training. Cardio-vascular work will improve your heart and lungs, but only power training builds the sheer strength and physical toughness that goes with being truly fit.

Arnie Schwarzenegger is an excellent example of the results of an enormous amount of power training (and, alas, some steroid abuse when he was younger). His incredible physique has been developed to the upper limits by the careful use of weight-training routines designed to maximize muscle bulk (and therefore strength), combined with a diet formulated to assist the process. Not that Schwarzenegger would be likely to pass SAS selection; watch him try to run in any of his films, and you will soon see that his physique hampers the movement of his legs. Having trained his body for strength and bulk, Schwarzenegger is not built for endurance – although I imagine that he would be very fast over short distances because of his immense muscle power.

Achieving a Balance

A soldier who turned up for SAS selection or P-Company without having achieved the right balance between power and endurance would be in for a lot of heartache. Without the cardio-vascular endurance to run for 10 miles or march for 40, he's not going to make it; but without the strength in his back and shoulders, he's not going to be able to carry the loads. In normal life as well, sticking to one form of exercise is unsatisfactory. You will always get more benefit from a balanced, all-round programme if you wish to achieve a better level of health and fitness.

> If you exercise first thing in the morning, directly after getting out of bed, you must be sure to pay particular attention to your warm-up. You may need to wait for 30 minutes or so for your metabolism to get going, and you will find that your muscles have contracted overnight and your joints have stiffened a little. Don't be tempted to leap straight from your bed into a hard workout because you will almost certainly injure yourself.

THE FIGHTING FIT WARM-UP AND STRETCH-OFF

BEFORE YOU START taking exercise of any sort, it is absolutely vital that you warm yourself up properly, stretching off the major muscles that you're going to use and raising your heart rate. If you don't, the chances are that you will end up with cramps, pulled or torn muscles and even stress fractures. Similarly, you should always warm down after each session, which allows your muscles to contract more gently. The following routine will get you ready for any of the exercises or workouts described in *Fighting Fit*. Always do it at the start of your workouts *and* at the end. And even after you've warmed up, always start exercising gently and build up gradually to full pace. Remember: if you get injured, you won't be able to train at all.

Head and Neck

Start your warm-up by rotating your head from side to side as far as it will go, then nod backwards and forwards – again as far as your head will go.

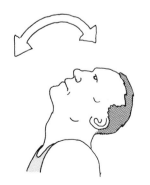

Shoulders

Roll your shoulders forwards as if shrugging, then do the same thing backwards. Hold your arms out to your sides at shoulder height, and then push your elbows back as far as they will go, as if you were trying to make them touch behind your back.

THE FIGHTING FIT WARM-UP
AND STRETCH-OFF

Trunk

With your arms held out to your sides at shoulder height, rotate your entire upper body to the left and then to the right, as far as you can comfortably go. Put your hands on your hips and rotate your entire pelvic area to the left and right, as if making an obscene gesture.

Legs

Stand with your feet shoulder-width apart. Without locking your knees, now try to touch the ground in front of, between and behind your feet with your fingertips. Don't force yourself if you can't quite manage it. Next, stand on one leg, grasp the opposite ankle in your hand and try to pull it up behind you so that your heel pushes into your buttock, then swop over and repeat the exercise with the other leg.

... And Finally

Gently jog around for a couple of minutes, stretching any muscles that feel stiff or tight. Remember to start exercising at an easy pace and, if any muscles feel sore, back off and stretch before trying to work them again.

THE FOLLOWING PAGES show you the basic strength exercises that you will be using for the Fighting Fit programmes. Half of them require no special equipment, but the rest require the use of weights or a 'multigym' which automatically introduces an element of risk. **Don't start the exercises until you know what you are doing!** If you are not already familiar with weight-training equipment, then get someone who is to show you what to do.

Getting Started

Some of the exercises which follow don't require any extra gear, but others do. If you want to go the whole hog and become super fighting fit, you're inevitably going to have to use a gym, but in fact all you really need is a multigym machine or similar – anything else is a bonus. The army, not surprisingly, have a lot of weight-training gear and I've never yet been to an army base which didn't have, at least, a multigym. If you don't have access to a gym in this way, there may well be a sports centre near you with a gym or 'conditioning room' where you can use good-quality equipment under professional supervision.

Grunting Poseurs

The downside of using gyms is that they are often filled with obscenely over-developed body-builders, grunting, sweating and mooching around in hideously revealing clothes, admiring themselves in the mirrors. Although these sad, side-show freaks think that they own any gym they spend more than ten minutes in, they are normally quite harmless and spend most of their time thinking about the next deliciously nutritious glass of raw egg and carrot purée.

Gear for Weight Training

A T-shirt, shorts and running shoes are perfectly adequate clothing for weight training. You may find that a pair of weight-training gloves helps to prevent callouses and blisters on your hands, and some people use a wide belt to support their back during workouts. That's all you need – but just read through any fitness magazine to see how the flimflam piles up to neck height when someone is trying to sell you workout clothes.

Alternative Weights

If you don't have weights at home, or access to a multigym, there are a number of alternatives that you can experiment with. Instead of dumb-bells you could try using books, baked bean tins or house bricks; as an alternative to a bar-bell try a suitably weighted sports bag, or even a strong broomstick with weighted containers attached to the ends. If you do use alternative weights, you must ensure that all of the components are very securely attached to prevent them from falling on you and that the weights are not going to shift about inside their containers as you use them, which might throw you off balance.

Many people find that training with weights reduces their flexibility and agility. Counteract this by spending the last 10 minutes of your weight workouts and multigym circuits stretching all of the muscles that you have been using, take a warm shower or bath and try to keep moving around for 20 minutes or so when you've finished. Avoid the temptation (however great it might be!) to collapse in an exhausted heap.

CHEST EXERCISES

1 Press-Ups

Anyone can do these. At home, in the office, in the bus queue – you can do press-ups anywhere and there are few better ways of improving the chest and arms. Lie face down on the ground, put the palms of your hands flat on the ground underneath your shoulders, stiffen your back and legs, and raise your body up, pivoting on your toes. Keep your back straight throughout the exercise and do it slowly and deliberately in sets of 20–40, depending on your fitness level.

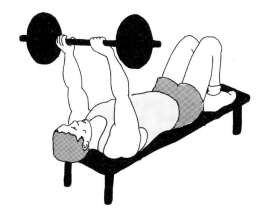

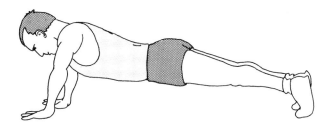

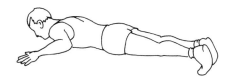

2 Bench Press

You need a multigym or a bar-bell, loaded with a weight that you can comfortably bench-press 12 times, and a bench to lie on. Lie on your back on the bench with your shoulders directly underneath the weights, ensuring that your back remains flat on the bench by lifting your feet off the ground and crossing your legs. Grip the bar (or handles on a multigym) with your hands shoulder-width apart and push it slowly and deliberately to the furthest extent of your arms, then slowly lower it back again. Do it 20 times (yes, I said 20).

If you are using a multigym, always carry a towel or cloth with you to clean the sweat off the equipment after each exercise, or during it if you are worried about slipping. There is nothing better designed to put you off exercising than lying in a pool of cold perspiration, and it is a ripe breeding ground for bugs like the athlete's foot fungus. You may also make a few friends with your obvious public spirit!

CHEST EXERCISES

3 Dips

You need two parallel bars about 2 ft (60 cm) apart and about 4 ft (1.2 m) off the ground, though the backs of two sturdy chairs would do just as well. Stand between the bars, grip one with each hand and lift yourself off the ground until your arms lock straight. Cross your legs and raise your feet to keep them out of the way. Now, lower yourself until your upper arms are parallel with the bars, then raise yourself up and lock your arms straight again – try to do 20 of these (they are very difficult at first).

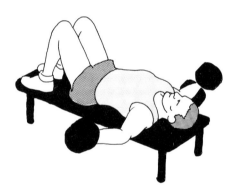

4 Lateral Raise

Lie flat on a bench holding two equally weighted dumb-bells, one in each hand, together above your chest. With your elbows slightly bent, lower them to your sides, then raise them again to the starting position. Use a weight that allows you to do about 20 repetitions (reps).

5 Pullovers

You can do these with either a bar-bell or two equally weighted dumb-bells. Lie on a narrow, flat bench holding the weight at arm's length above your chest, then, keeping your arms straight, lower the weight(s) behind your head while breathing in. Finally, bring the weight back to the starting position as you exhale. Use a weight which allows you to do 12 reps comfortably – but do 20.

6 Chins

You need a bar to hang from about 6 ft 6 in (2 m) off the ground. Grip the bar with your hands slightly more than shoulder-width apart, and hang from it with your legs crossed and your feet tucked behind you. Slowly and deliberately raise yourself until you can touch the bar with the bridge of your nose, then slowly lower yourself down again. Build up to being able to do this in sets of 12 reps (like dips, these are very difficult at first).

7 Hyperextensions

Lie face down on the floor with your hands behind your head, then raise your chest and shoulders as far as you can off the floor and lower them again – you should be able to do sets of at least 30 of these. Avoid hooking your feet under any stationary object as you will end up training your legs more than your back.

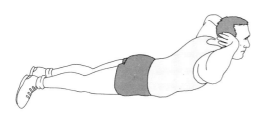

8 Bent Over Rowing

You need either a bar-bell or two equally weighted dumb-bells for this. With your feet shoulder-width apart, bend over and grip the weight(s). Stay bent over while pulling the weight to your waist, then lower back to the ground. Use a weight that allows you to do sets of 12.

9 The Good Morning Exercise

God knows why it's called this. Hold a bar-bell across your shoulders while standing up straight, then bend forward from the waist until your body is parallel to the floor. Finish by straightening again, using the muscles in the small of your back. Use a weight that allows you to do sets of 12.

SHOULDERS

10 Shoulder Press

This exercise is best done on a multigym in the seated position with your back supported, but it can just as easily be performed standing with a bar-bell. Hold the weight-bar in position at the back of the neck with your hands slightly more than shoulder-width apart, then slowly and deliberately push the bar directly upwards before lowering it again. Do sets of 12 reps.

11 Dumb-Bell Press

Stand with your back straight and your feet shoulder-width apart, holding an equally weighted dumb-bell at each shoulder. Alternately raise each one above your head. Do 18 in each set. Easy, isn't it?

12 Side Lateral Raise

Stand straight with your feet shoulder-width apart, holding an equally weighted dumb-bell in each hand at your waist. Keeping your arms straight, simultaneously raise the dumb-bells away from your body to shoulder height, then lower. Do sets of 12.

13 Bent Lateral Raise

This is the same as the last exercise, the side lateral raise, except that you bend forwards and lift the weights from a position below you rather than at your sides. Do sets of 12.

14 Curls

Hold a bar-bell, or the curling bar from a multigym, at your waist, with your elbows locked in to your sides. Keep your feet shoulder-width apart and your back straight, then 'curl' the bar up to your shoulders and back again. Do 20 reps in a set.

16 Concentration Curls

Sit on a bench with a single dumb-bell clutched in one hand. Rest your elbow on your leg, keeping the other arm out of the way, and slowly curl the dumb-bell to your shoulder, then slowly lower it. Do this in sets of 12.

15 Tricep Dips

You need two stable benches about 4 ft (1.2 m) apart. Adopt a sitting position with your feet on one bench and your bum on the other. Take your weight on your hands and slide your body forward so that your bottom is clear to drop below the level of the bench. Lower yourself until your upper arms are parallel to the ground, then straighten them. Do this in sets of 20.

17 Press Downs

These can only easily be done on a multigym or similar machine which has a bar for pulling down. Stand in front of the machine with the bar clasped in both hands in front of your chest and your elbows locked, as far as possible, into your sides. Press the bar down, using only your arm muscles, until your arms are straight in front of you, then allow the bar to rise to its starting position. Do 15 reps in each set.

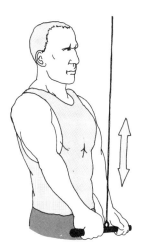

ABDOMEN

Note: When doing exercises for the abs you should always avoid locking your feet under anything. Doing this makes the exercise easier, but your legs do all the work and you put unnecessary strain on the lower back.

18 Crunches

Lie on your back with your legs bent, your feet flat on the floor and your hands behind your head. Raise your upper body as if trying to touch your knees with your elbows. When you have 'crunched' up as far as you can, pause before lowering your body down. The movement is not as large as for a traditional 'sit-up' but it is far better for you.

19 Leg Raises

Lie flat on your back with your hands under your bum. Keeping your legs straight and pointing your toes daintily, raise your feet 6 in (15 cm) off the ground. This is the start position. Now raise your feet from 6 to about 18 in (45 cm) off the ground, then back to 6 again. Keep your feet off the ground throughout the exercise and do 30 in a set.

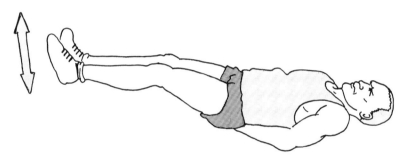

20 V-Crunches

Lie on your back with your hands behind your head and your knees slightly bent. Crunch your upper body as for normal crunches, but bring your knees up as well and touch your knees to your elbows. Do sets of 25.

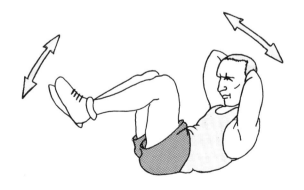

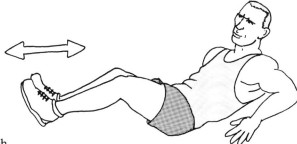

21 Seated Leg Push

Ideally you should be sitting on the edge of a bench, but you can do these on the floor as well. Sit upright with your hands supporting you next to your bottom. To perform the exercise, bring your knees to your chest then straighten your legs out, but without allowing your feet to touch the ground throughout the set. Try to do 35–40 in a set.

22 Crossover Crunches

These are performed as for V-Crunches, but alternately touching your right elbow to your left knee and vice versa. Do them in sets of 20.

For weight training to work, your body needs a good supply of the male hormone testosterone. This means that women respond to weight training less well than men and children get little or no benefit.

Remember

The 22 exercises described here are basic but highly beneficial. If, after reading this book and looking at the pictures, you are unsure how to do any of them, ask an instructor at your gym to show you. If you feel severe pain at any stage while doing them, stop immediately – you may have pulled a muscle or worse. In any event, don't try any of them until you are sure you know what you are doing.

The best person to show you how to perform weights exercises is an instructor on the spot. Small variations in posture can mean the difference between strong muscles and pulled muscles. Don't let your enthusiasm get the better of you; if you perform weight exercises carefully, you can't fail to improve.

2 BASIC TRAINING

RUNNING

THERE ARE NO two ways about it, anyone who wants to join the SAS or Paras is going to end up running many miles, both in training and on the courses themselves. And since the mid-1970s, when the fitness boom began, running has become the premier activity for aspiring fitties everywhere. The reasons are simple: running is a very efficient way of getting fit, it's easy and cheap, and it's flexible.

The Pluses

Running is a straightforward aerobic exercise. As you pound along you raise your heart rate, increase your oxygen intake and heighten the flow of blood to the parts of your body being used, with all the benefits that this creates. You also increase the rate at which you use the energy which is stored in your body and start to draw upon your reserves of fat (which is why you lose weight). Finally, running strengthens the muscles of your legs and back, and it helps to build up your joints.

The Minuses

Disadvantages to running are few. If you are in good health, the only difficulty that you are likely to encounter is the normal wear and tear that running imposes on your body. This can include blisters, muscle strains and slightly more serious conditions like shin splints, stress fractures and joint damage. In fairness, these are more often than not caused by poor running form, obesity, and trying to do too much too soon.

Running Style and Form

The human body is designed for running and anyone in normal health can do it. Unfortunately, though, it is easy to get into bad habits and these can cause problems. So, if you are taking up running after years of inactivity, or just want to make a fresh start, here are some pointers on style and form.

Posture

Your posture when you run should be upright but relaxed, perhaps leaning slightly forwards. If you lean too far forward, you have to work harder to stay upright; lean too far back, on the other hand, and you exert a braking effect on your movements.

Arm Action

What you do with your arms when you run is nearly as important as how you use your legs. Look at a sprinter like Linford Christie; he has massively developed arms and shoulders which he uses to help propel himself forward. When you run, you should try to ensure that your arms are relaxed; they should stay between your waistline and your chest. If you let them swing around too loosely, the rest of your upper body will follow and you will lose forward momentum – and the same thing will happen if you hold your arms too rigidly.

Footstrike

There is a lot of debate among runners about footstrike, mainly because some of the best long-distance athletes use the 'wrong' sort. The most comfortable and efficient footstrike that the average runner can adopt is to go 'heel-ball'. This means that you hit the ground with the outside edge of your heel, pivot through your foot and take off for the next step from the ball of your foot. Some people seem to slap along on their feet, making a hell of a racket, and in my experience these are the ones who get joint and bone injuries. If you find that you're running too heavily, you will have to make a very conscious effort to correct yourself.

The average semi-serious runner, as opposed to occasional jogger, runs between 20 and 25 miles per week, taking between 7 and 9 minutes to cover each mile. Don't be fooled by people who claim to run 10 miles every day; the chances are that they're kidding themselves more than you. Almost 70–80 miles per week would be a good target for an Olympic long-distance runner, but it is way beyond the capabilities of the average fitness enthusiast.

RUNNING

HOW FAR SHOULD you run in a session and how fast? Very good questions, because it is all too easy to settle into a groove of doing too little, or even too much, and so miss the full benefit of the training time and the commitment that you are making. So much depends on your level of fitness, build and innumerable other factors. The clever answer is that you should be running hard enough to get your heart rate into the aerobic training range (between 65 and 75 per cent of your maximum) for at least 30 minutes, at least three times per week – which is fine if you're just looking for a steady improvement in aerobic fitness over the long term. However, by varying the sort of running that you do, the distances that you cover and the intensity at which you run them, you can improve far more quickly than by grinding out the same distances in the same times day after day. Specific workouts for speed training – intervals, fartlek and hills – are covered in Chapters 3 and 5.

The Fighting Fit Runs

For the Fighting Fit programmes we will be using three different types of run: a short, faster session, a medium-distance 'basic' run and a long, slow endurance-builder. How far and how fast you should go depends on how fit you are, so the following are guidelines only. Once you start training in earnest, you will gain a feel for exactly how much value you get from each workout and thus be able to judge the intensity at which you should run.

Running for Time

It always annoys me to hear some racing-snake yammering on about how he's just completed a 12-miler, or about the 60 miles he did last week – I will never be a great long-distance runner and I find it disheartening to be compared to someone who is. The answer is to measure your runs in terms of time, not distance. There are two advantages in this: first, you won't become hung up about mileages (which can push you into over-training) and, secondly, you maintain a consistency of quality because as you become fitter and faster, thus covering particular distances more quickly,

you are nonetheless running for the same time and so will go farther. If you restrict yourself to covering set distances, it is all too easy to succumb to the temptation of staying with a particular route for too long, so that a 6-mile run which started off taking you, say, 45 minutes can easily end up lasting only 38, thereby knocking 7 minutes of quality training out of your programme.

The Short Fast Run

The shortest basic run you will do in the Fighting Fit programmes is for 30 minutes. You would do a maximum of two of these per week, on a day when you might be taking some other form of exercise. The pace should be fast: if you run this workout with a partner, you shouldn't be able to talk to him (or her), but nor should you be sprinting. For me, the pace of a run like this is about 6 minutes per mile – but you may well want to go faster or slower. Don't get up to full pace until you've been running for about 5 or 6 minutes or you will go into oxygen debt and 'tie up'.

The Basic Run

The standard run lasts for 45 minutes at a comfortable, steady pace. Running with a friend, you should be able to talk to each other, but only just – don't expect to be able to hold a symposium on Aristotelian metaphysics during this workout. My average pace for this run is about 7 minutes per mile on a good day, but you can slow things down slightly and take on a few gentle hills if you have any available.

The Endurance Builder

The last of the three basic runs is the Endurance Builder. This is 90 minutes of slow, gentle jogging at a pace where you could hold a comfortable conversation with a running partner. You might well only do this run once a fortnight, moving to once a week as you get fitter, because, although it is slow, you will certainly feel it afterwards.

SWIMMING

THE GREAT ADVANTAGE of swimming over most other forms of aerobic exercise is that it places demands on all parts of the body, not just on the heart and lungs. Not only does swimming increase your endurance, it also acts as a superb conditioner for the upper body. At the same time, because water supports your body, there is very little stress on your bones and joints which means that injuries are rare. If you are looking to do P-Company, the Commando course or SAS selection, you should consider swimming as a supplement to running because you won't pass the courses without

the leg strength that running provides. On the other hand, if you are simply trying to improve your fitness and you don't like running, swimming can be substituted minute for minute.

Swimming Equipment

All you need for swimming is a costume and a pool. If your eyes are sensitive or you wear contact lenses, you should consider investing in a pair of goggles. I haven't got any great preferences for swimming cossies, though

SWIMMING

I imagine that those which are specially made for swimming races are probably pretty good – they certainly show off your package if you like that sort of thing.

The Basics

If you can't swim, you will have real difficulty learning from a book. Your best course of action will be to head off to your local pool and book yourself some lessons – I've yet to visit a pool where there isn't an instructor – which will enable you to start with some confidence. The two strokes that you will need to know are the front crawl and breast-stroke; other strokes are useful but they are only the icing on the cake. Once you learn how to swim, you never forget – it's like knowing how to walk.

How Far and How Fast?

My own swimming workouts tend to be fairly unimaginative, because I use swimming as a supplementary exercise to running and gym work. Normally I just swim continuously up and down the pool for 30 minutes or so, usually doing breast-stroke, sometimes alternating breast-stroke with front crawl. If you have similar limited aims in mind, and can stand the boredom, there's no reason why you shouldn't do the same – it's a perfectly good way of exercising. There are some far more interesting swimming workouts, however, and these are outlined below. A point to note is that your training heart rate is likely to be about 15 to 20 beats per minute slower than when taking other forms of exercise, because, being horizontal, your heart doesn't have to work as hard getting the blood around your body.

Pyramid Swimming

An excellent way of building up endurance is by swimming 'pyramids'. An example of this might be a '5' in which you swim 1 length, followed by a set rest period (say, 20 seconds), then 2 lengths with the same rest period and so on up to 5, then down again to 1. In total this comes to 25 lengths which in a 25-metre pool is 625 metres, a bit more than a third of a mile. Swimming an '8' in a 25-metre pool (1–2–3–4–5–6–7–8–7–6–5–4–3–2–1) adds up to 1,600 metres, about a mile. An advantage of this workout is that the short rest periods help you to maintain your speed without letting your heart rate drop out of the training range.

Interval Swims

Interval swimming not only builds endurance but helps with speed as well. Interval training comprises a timed swim alternated with a timed rest. Once you have gained confidence as a swimmer, start to time yourself to see how quickly you can do certain distances. You may find that you can do 100 metres in 4 minutes; if so, try intervals of 4 minutes 30 seconds – this means that you give yourself four and a half minutes to swim 100 metres *and* take a rest before doing the next 100 metres. Put the intervals into sets of 4 (4 x 100 metres) and build up the number of sets that you can do, awarding yourself a couple of minutes' rest between each set. As the weeks go by, your times will start to improve, giving you more rest between each interval; when this happens, shorten your time allowance – remember, you don't want your heart rate to drop out of the training range.

Eating and Drinking

When I was a kid I was told that if I ate before I went swimming I would get stomach cramps and drown. This has been tested scientifically and is a load of old bollocks. Having said that, it isn't ever comfortable to exercise on a full stomach, so avoid eating much for an hour or two before swimming. However, it is worth drinking some water both before and after swimming – the reason being that you sweat just as much as when you are taking other forms of exercise, only you don't notice it. A glass or two of water, or some other soft drink, will prevent dehydration.

> Swimmers are in the fortunate position of being able to take a much heavier training load for much longer because their body-weight is partially offset by buoyancy. This means that it is an activity that can be continued well into old age and in spite of physical disability. What's more, swimming genuinely exercises the parts that other sports cannot reach.

CYCLING, WALKING AND AEROBICS

Cycling

An alternative to running, which also uses the big leg muscles, is cycling. Its main benefit in comparison to running is that, like swimming, it is largely impact-free. This helps reduce your chances of getting injured. On the other hand, cycling does very little for the muscles of the upper body, can be dangerous (you can't easily fall off a swimming pool) and requires you to lash out a lot of dosh on a decent bike. As with all aerobic exercises, you need to get your heart rate into the training range for at least half an hour to make it worthwhile. This can be difficult in a town because of traffic. Ideally, your cycle route should consist of a country road or park with plenty of hills to help build up leg strength – or you can go to a gym and use an exercise bike with variable resistance.

Cycling Rhythm

The rhythm that you should aim to achieve while cycling is about 80 turns of the pedal per minute. If your bike has gears, this will probably mean that you can't use your top gears except when going down hills (using the top gear on flat surfaces increases strain on the knee joints by a considerable amount and can cause injury). The best way of judging if you are at the right speed or not is as follows: if your legs become tired before you get out of breath, you are in too high a gear and are using your leg muscles too much, whereas if you get out of breath but your legs remain strong, your gears are too low.

The ultimate all-round endurance sport is triathlon; combining swimming, cycling and running it is a challenge for anyone who likes to keep fit, from occasional fun runners to Olympic athletes. The greatest triathlon challenge is the Ironman in Hawaii – a 2.4 mile (3.8 km) sea swim followed by a 112 mile (180 km) bike ride followed by a full 26 mile (42 km) marathon. Astoundingly enough, the best times for this event are well under eight and a half hours.

CYCLING, WALKING AND AEROBICS

Walking

The only difference between walking a distance and running it, I have been told, is the time it takes you to do it. In terms of energy used and muscle strength gained, this may well be so, though I doubt if there is a direct comparison in cardio-vascular improvement. If you are training for SAS selection, you are going to have to get used to a lot of walking, over hills and carrying a rucksack, but that is different from the exercise walking advocated by a number of gurus nowadays. Personally, I find it hard to take seriously the sight of grown men and women striding round my local park wearing lurex tights and determined expressions. There is no doubt that walking improves your fitness, but by nothing like the factor that you will achieve by running, swimming or cycling.

Aerobics

Like walking, aerobics – of the kind practised at lunch-time classes – undoubtedly makes you feel better. As a form of exercise, however, it is going to leave you a long way off the standards you'll reach on a Fighting Fit programme. Don't neglect it altogether, though, as the most enjoyable aerobic exercise of all is good old bonking. It would be extremely difficult to get your heart rate into the training range for a full 30 minutes, but you can have a lot of fun trying. I would suggest using the more athletic positions, possibly in a hammock, to give yourself the best shot at it (*warning: don't let your partner catch you measuring your heart rate during sex as this may seriously damage your health*).

If your natural running style is comfortable for you and doesn't cause injuries, don't attempt to change it. Many people have slightly unequal legs or arms which cause them to look strange when they run but which don't affect their performance. The chances are that your natural style is the best way for you as an individual. We can't all be marathon champions, and remember the old army proverb: 'If it ain't broke, don't fix it.'

CHAPTER 3
COMBINED OPERATIONS

INTERVAL TRAINING

INTERVAL TRAINING is a method of gaining speed and leg strength without having to use weight-training equipment. A proper interval workout will leave you a quivering, sweat-soaked mess, but the gains that you make are quite extraordinary. All you need to wear is your normal running kit and the only other requirement is somewhere to run.

The principle behind interval training is that you exercise hard, then recover just enough to repeat the exercise, over and over again during a relatively short period. To get the best results, the distance that you run should remain consistent and, consequently, athletes generally do interval sessions on a proper running track. This is by no means essential, because you can get equally good results running around the outside of a football or rugby pitch, or along a path where trees or lamp-posts are evenly spaced.

The First Interval Session

For your first interval session, try running 8 × 100 metres. This means that you will be sprinting for 100 metres exactly 8 times, with a measured rest period between each sprint. If you are using a running track it will be divided into four quarters of 100 metres each; if you are using a football pitch it will be about 100 metres long; while on a path or road select two objects that are 100 metres apart. All you have to do is this: once you have warmed up, go to the start of your first 100-metre stretch and sprint, at 100 per cent effort, to the end of the leg. Now jog the next 100 metres, taking not more than 60 seconds, sprint the next 100 and so on, until you have completed 8 sprints and 8 jogs. It sounds easy, but by the end of the session you will be wishing that you'd taken up knitting instead.

Building Up

As your fitness improves, you will be able to handle a much greater workload during interval sessions and you can experiment with much greater distances. For example, middle- and long-distance runners will often run intervals sets of a mile or more, repeated perhaps ten times as part of their training. While this is unnecessary for most people, a session of 8 × 400 metres is certainly worth a try.

Speed workouts take much more out of you than normal running. If you find that you aren't recovering from them quickly enough, shift your speed workout day so that it falls before a day off training. As you become stronger you will be more able to cope with it in the midst of your normal training.

Pace

Interval running is usually done at 100 per cent, but this doesn't mean that you have to sprint at the same speed for 400 metres as you would over 100 metres. Use a speed appropriate for the distance that you've got to travel, but remember that you'll be able to go faster and faster as the weeks go by.

Frequency

Interval training helps you make large improvements to your fitness, but it takes a lot out of you. Don't try to do more than one interval session a week at first and never do more than two unless you are training for something very speed-specific.

You can simplify a fartlek workout by imposing some rules on yourself. Find an undulating course and, after you've jogged for 10 minutes or so to warm up, run at normal pace on the flat, at 80 per cent effort on long hills, 100 per cent effort on short hills and jog the downhill stretches. You should find that this balances itself out and removes the requirement for all that complicated thinking.

FARTLEK IS A SWEDISH word meaning 'speed play', but fartlek running is a training technique that sits in between interval training and normal running as a means of building up leg strength. Once again, it requires no special equipment other than normal running gear and a place to run.

Fartlek Technique

A fartlek workout is normally done over your usual running routes. The technique consists of little more than constant changes of pace, combined, if possible, with running up and down a few hills. Typically, you might run the first mile at a fairly easy pace before moving up to 80 per cent of full effort for two minutes, then a jog for a minute, then 100 per cent effort for a minute, then 30 seconds of walking and so on. In this way, an aerobic run is combined with a strength session.

Messing Around

You need to make a plan before you start a fartlek session because it's very easy to end up doing 90 per cent of the session at a gentle jog with a couple of sprints thrown in. Either exercise some self-discipline or run with a partner or in a small group – probably the most enjoyable way to do a fartlek session anyway. The best location for fartlek running is the countryside, or in a park or golf-course (if you can get permission),

where you have a variety of different surfaces to run on, together with hills, trees, fresh air and all the rest of it. Lovely!

If you plan to do a 30-minute fartlek run, the break-down would look something like this:

1	5 minutes of jogging to warm up
2	2 minutes at 80 per cent of full pace
3	2 minutes at normal running pace
4	30 seconds at 100 per cent pace
5	30 seconds at a slow jog
6	2 minutes at 80 per cent
7	1 minute at 100 per cent
8	2 minutes of jogging
9	1 minute walking
10	2 minutes at normal pace
11	2 minutes at 80 per cent
12	30 seconds at 100 per cent
13	30 seconds at a slow jog
14	2 minutes at 80 per cent
15	1 minute at normal pace
16	1 minute at 100 per cent
17	5 minutes of jogging (warm down)

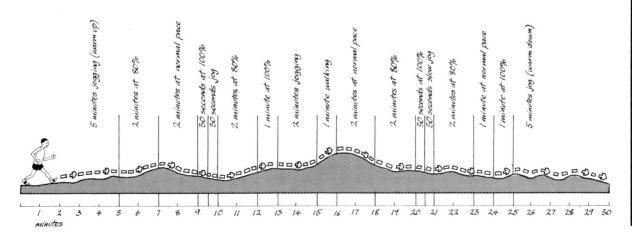

5 minutes jogging (warm up) · 2 minutes at 80% · 2 minutes at normal pace · 30 seconds at 100% · 30 seconds jog · 2 minutes at 80% · 1 minute at 100% · 2 minutes jogging · 1 minute walking · 2 minutes at normal pace · 2 minutes at 80% · 30 seconds at 100% · 30 seconds slow jog · 2 minutes at 80% · 1 minute at normal pace · 1 minute at 100% · 5 minutes jog (warm down)

1 2 3 4 5 6 7 8 9 10 11 12 13 14 15 16 17 18 19 20 21 22 23 24 25 26 27 28 29 30
minutes

3 COMBINED OPERATIONS

THE MACHINE WORKOUT

MULTIGYM, UNIVERSAL, NAUTILUS and all the other fitness machines have proved, by and large, to be a great help to those in search of fitness. A lot of the effort involved in shifting dumb-bells and bar-bells around is expended in balancing and controlling them. This may contribute to muscle growth for body-builders and the like, but the downside is that free weights are considerably more dangerous than a machine. If you get into trouble bench-pressing on a fitness machine, the weight is unlikely to fall on you – whereas with a free weight that could just happen.

Using Machines

It is not possible to give a detailed workout programme because fitness machines vary so much, but using a machine is the same as doing any other kind of weights exercise. The gains that you make are governed entirely by the number of repetitions that you do, the amount of weight that you shift on each repetition and the number of sets that you manage.

Designing a Circuit

There are, essentially, two types of fitness machine: integrated multi-exercise machines of the multigym kind, and specialized single-exercise machines. On a multigym, you can perform one exercise or more at each 'station', and the machines are generally designed so that you can start anywhere and then go to every station in turn, performing as many reps as you need. This also means that more than one person can use the machine at the same time. You can train like that, and many people do, but you may not get the best results. It is now quite widely accepted that you will achieve the best results by training each part of your body in turn, doing several different exercises for each part. Multi-exercise machines don't really encourage you to do this. To get the maximum effect from them, don't be fooled into doing a straight circuit – pick and choose from the menu of exercises on offer.

The sequence for a weight-training circuit is Chest, Shoulders, Back, Arms, Legs, Abdominals. The box on the opposite page is a suggested circuit which should be possible using a typical multi-exercise machine and a bit of clear floor space. Use this circuit when you're doing the Fighting Fit programmes:

Don't use the 'sit-up' station on exercise machines to do the abdominal exercises because you normally lock your feet under a bar which puts a lot of strain on your back. Always keep your feet free when exercising the stomach muscles.

A Multigym Circuit

Exercise	Number of Reps	Exercise	Number of Reps
Press-Ups	25	Curls	20
Bench Press	20	Press Downs	15
Dips	20	Crunches	25
Chins	12	Leg Raises	30
Hyperextensions	30	V-Crunches	25
Bent Over Rowing	12	Seated Leg Push	35
Shoulder Press	12	Crossover Crunches	20

3 COMBINED OPERATIONS

AEROBIC SUPER CIRCUITS

YOU WILL FIND 'super circuits' in one form or another at most sports centres and gyms. Super circuits are, normally, an organized group session which combines the best aspects of aerobics with weight exercises in a fun format with some loud music thrown in. All the super circuits that I've been to have included a good warm-up at the start and, just as importantly, an organized warm down afterwards. Even better news is that some sports centres have bars where you can have a beer or two after the session, safe in the knowledge that it isn't going to go straight to your waistline.

The Aim

Nobody does super circuits for building muscle bulk, but what you should expect to achieve is an increase in both local muscular and cardio-vascular endurance. Consequently, the weights that you lift should be lighter than you would normally go for and you should try to do far more repetitions. You are normally helped in this by the fact that the sessions are done to music and divided up into sections about a minute long. You alternate between using a weight and bouncing about doing some aerobic exercise, trying to pack as many reps as possible into a minute.

Beware!

A word of warning about group super circuits – anyone can go to them! This can mean that some terrifying-looking people dressed up in lurex will be wobbling around. Don't fall into this trap yourself – if you're a bit overweight, wear a bulky T-shirt and a pair of shorts. You'll look a lot better and you will be a whole lot more comfortable.

You can seriously increase the intensity of a weight circuit by cutting the amount of rest that you allow yourself between each exercise. By doing this, you may be able to get your heart rate into the aerobic training range throughout your workout. Top martial arts exponents regularly use this technique because their sport requires a combination of enormous strength with extended endurance. But be careful to wait until you are quite fit before you try this; they aren't known as 'heart attack sessions' for nothing!

CHAPTER 4
FITNESS FUEL

FOOD FACTS

THIS CHAPTER IS about the kinds of food that you should, and shouldn't, be eating. If you don't have to cook for yourself – if, for example, you're married and your partner cooks, you still live with your mum, or you're a single soldier living in barracks – here is a guide to what sorts of food are good fitness fuel and what aren't. And if you do cook, there is a complete set of fourteen days' worth of easy recipes, together with two shopping lists and some suggestions on how to get on with the cooking.

A lot of people still feel that being able to cook properly is pretty wet, that it is a black art taught to little girls at their mother's knee (or some other low joint) – what a load of old bollocks! There's a saying in the army that 'Any idiot can be uncomfortable', meaning that if you aren't prepared to look after yourself properly, then you have nobody to blame but yourself. Anyone with two brain cells to rub together can learn to cook some pretty good food – all you have to do is follow a recipe in a cookbook, use the correct ingredients and Bob's your uncle! But the recipes in this chapter have been devised especially for people with just one brain cell sparking away on its own; they are all very healthy and they don't take long to prepare – so give them a try.

This is *not* a calorie-controlled diet. There are only fourteen days' worth of food here, and you may find yourself getting a little bored if you repeat the recipes week after week. The important thing is that you learn how to choose, prepare and eat the right sorts of food and stop eating the crap.

I have to admit that I didn't devise any of the recipes myself. I like cooking and following recipes, but I'm not up to creating them. Instead, they were provided for me by Caroline Mercer, a professional cook whom I've known for years. I asked her to come up with meals that are high in carbohydrates and fibre, low in fat, easy to cook, tasty and filling.

How to Use This Chapter

Apart from the section at the end on special food supplements, this chapter is about a complete diet for fourteen days, conveniently organized into two sections of seven days each. For each week there is a complete shopping list which covers everything on the diet for that week for one person; and when I say everything, I mean everything – like Old Mother Hubbard, I'm assuming that the cupboard is completely bare. Check the contents of your fridge and larder against the shopping list because you may well have a lot of the ingredients already. The shopping list is designed so that you will have to make only one visit to a reasonably sized supermarket each week.

There is a selection of breakfasts and lunches for you to choose from, together with instructions on how to make salads and prepare vegetables to go with the evening meals. The evening meals themselves are given after the shopping lists, and I have included an entire suggested menu for each week as a quick reference.

Finally, the equipment that you need is basic. You should easily be able to cook it all on a stove with a couple of rings, a grill and an oven. You will need a small selection of pots and pans, a sharp knife and a wooden spoon or two.

THIS IS A brief introduction to the different types of food that we eat and what their benefits are.

Carbohydrates

Carbohydrates are the most efficient source of energy for people who take a lot of exercise and the food that you eat should contain lots of them. Foods which are high in carbohydrates include:

CARBOHYDRATES
Pasta – spaghetti, ravioli, lasagne, etc.
Starchy vegetables – potatoes, rice, etc.
Fruit
Bread
Pulses (peas, beans and lentils)

Fats

Apart from being a source of energy, fat is required by the body for a number of tasks, including the production of tissue and as insulation against heat and cold. Unfortunately, our normal Western diet contains too much fat and it ends up in hideous, wobbling lumps in all the wrong places. Fat should form no more than 15 per cent of your total food consumption, so in the long run you're better off avoiding foods which contain concealed fats such as:

FATS
Biscuits
Cakes
Chocolate
Mayonnaise
French fries

We all know what we shouldn't be eating. There is no harm in the occasional burger and fries, but if that's all your diet consists of then you are going to turn into a real porker!

Protein

Proteins are the basic building materials for our bodies, but like fat they shouldn't form more than 15 per cent of your diet. The reason for this is that excess proteins are either simply eliminated from the body as urine or they are stored as fat. Most diets which include the following will supply more than enough protein for the average person's requirements:

PROTEIN
Milk and milk products
Eggs
Pulses
Potatoes
Rice
Nuts
Lean meats

Water

You should always ensure that you are drinking plenty of fluids, particularly if you are doing a fitness programme. Dehydration markedly reduces your ability to exercise and can be dangerous. The best way to gauge whether you are drinking enough water is by examining your urine. It should be clear and any discoloration could be a sign of dehydration.

If you fed your dog the sort of food that the average European or American eats, it would become depressed, listless, fat and constipated: and it would be more likely to die young from heart disease or cancer. More thought has gone into the nutritional value of a can of pet food than into the typical Western diet.

4 FITNESS FUEL

Breakfast

One bowl of high-fibre cereal with skimmed milk and a sugar substitute to taste. Choose from brands such as All-Bran, Bran Flakes or Shredded Wheat.

plus

One slice of whole-wheat toast spread with Marmite or Vegemite or a low-sugar jam or marmalade. No butter or margarine to be used.

Once a week you may have a small grilled breakfast consisting of:

GUARDHOUSE GRILL
3 rashers of grilled lean back bacon
2 grilled tomatoes
Grilled mushrooms
I boiled or poached egg
I piece of fruit

Lunch

Choose any of the lunches described below. You can also eat a piece of fruit or a diet yoghurt each lunch-time. Remember – no butter on your bread.

MIDDAY MUNCHES
1   I boiled egg with 2 slices of whole-wheat toast.
2   A whole-wheat sandwich made from 2 slices of bread with 2 slices of lean ham or beef, some lettuce and some low-calorie mayonnaise.
3   Tuna fish salad made with a small can of tuna in brine, drained, combined with a quarter of a cucumber, sliced, 2 tomatoes, a handful of shredded lettuce and low-calorie mayonnaise.
4   A whole-wheat sandwich made with 2 slices of bread (dry), half a sliced chicken breast with the fat and skin removed, low-calorie mayonnaise, shredded lettuce and salt and pepper.
5   Jacket potato with a) low-fat pineapple cottage cheese and a small salad, or b) I slice of chopped lean ham, I teaspoon of mustard, I teaspoon of low-calorie mayonnaise and a small salad, or c) low-fat grated cheese with a handful of chopped chives and a small salad.
6   6 Ryvitas or similar spread with low-calorie mayonnaise or oil-free dressing, and either 2 slices of lean meat with shredded lettuce and sliced tomato, or half a sliced chicken breast (the fat and skin removed) with shredded lettuce and sliced tomato.
7   I piece of cold, cooked chicken (the fat and skin removed) with a mixed salad.
8   2 slices of dry whole-wheat toast with I small can of baked beans, warmed through.
9   2 slices of dry whole-wheat toast with I small can of tuna in brine, drained.
10   Mixed vegetable salad made with *raw* broccoli, cauliflower, mixed peppers, cucumber, tomato and mushrooms. Use oil-free dressing.
11   An omelette made with chopped vegetables and herbs, not cheese. Use 2 eggs. You should not eat this lunch more than once a week.

Cooking Methods

Steaming Any combination of vegetables will do, but vary the mixture so that you do not become bored. Peel and chop the vegetables as appropriate and place them in a sieve over a pan of boiling water, or in a steamer. Cover with a lid and boil until they are just tender but not soft. Keep an eye on the pan to ensure that it does not boil dry.

Stir frying As with steaming, vary the combination of vegetables. Lightly fry them in one tablespoon of olive oil. Season well with salt and pepper, adding dried or fresh herbs to taste.

Accompanying Evening Meals

Vegetables are much better steamed rather than boiled. In this way they keep both their taste and many of the vitamins and minerals that would otherwise be lost. You should get used to eating your vegetables slightly crunchy.

The best methods of cooking vegetables are listed in the opposite column.

Snacks

If you feel hungry between meals, a piece of fruit will fill the gap until you eat properly. Alternatively you could try a nut or muesli bar, but be warned: these contain lots of sugar and you certainly shouldn't eat more than one per day.

Cauliflower	Steam or stir fry
Broccoli	Steam or stir fry
Savoy Cabbage	Steam or stir fry (with caraway seeds)
Red Cabbage	Slice, then add a chopped apple, some sultanas and a glass of orange juice. Cook gently in a covered pan for about an hour. Add water if necessary.
Spinach	Wash, shake dry then wilt gently in a pan with no added water
Carrots	Steam or stir fry
Parsnips	Boil then mash with salt and pepper, or stir fry
Onions	Stir fry
Leeks	Steam or stir fry
Beans	Steam
Courgettes (zucchini)	Steam or stir fry
Peppers (red or green)	Steam or stir fry
Tomatoes	Halve and grill
Sweetcorn	Boil large cobs, or stir fry baby ones
Mushrooms	Stir fry, or as with many of the above eat raw

COOK'S TIPS

STEAM VEGETABLES BY PLACING THEM IN A METAL SIEVE OVER A PAN HALF FULL OF BOILING WATER (WITH THE LID ON!).

TASTE THEM FROM TIME TO TIME TO CHECK IF THEY ARE COOKED AND ALSO MAKE SURE THAT THE PAN DOESN'T BOIL DRY.

SALADS

To accompany lunches or evening meals

1 **Mixed Bean**
Slice and parboil a mixture of French beans and runner beans in boiling water for a couple of minutes, then rinse under cold water. Rinse half a can of kidney beans in cold water, mix with the other beans and add oil-free dressing.

2 **Mixed Lettuce**
It is more fun to use a variety of leaves, in different colours, including radiccio and chicory (endive). Add oil-free dressing and herbs to taste.

3 **Orange and Chicory (Endive) with Walnuts**
Slice 2 oranges with some sliced chicory (endive) and some walnuts.

4 **Tomato Salad**
Mix together a quartered tomato with some sliced cucumber and black olives.

5 **Beansprout and Orange**
Chop an orange and mix it with some bean sprouts. Stir in some oil-free dressing.

6 **Tomato and Fresh Basil**
Quarter some tomatoes and stir in some chopped fresh basil.

7 **Rice Salad**
Mix 8 oz (225 g) of cold, cooked brown rice with a chopped raw onion and some chopped red and green peppers. Use oil-free dressing.

8 **Carrot, Orange and Sultanas**
Grate a couple of carrots, add a handful of sultanas and a sliced orange. Moisten with orange juice.

9 **Cold Beetroot and Celery**
Dice the beetroot and mix with sliced celery. Add oil-free dressing.

10 **Celery, Apple and Pepper**
Slice the celery and mix with chopped red and green peppers and apples. Add low-calorie mayonnaise.

11 **Mixed Raw Vegetables**
Use a variety of vegetables in different colours such as broccoli, cauliflower, tomatoes, carrots, mushrooms and mangetout. Serve with oil-free dressing or low-calorie mayonnaise (add a crushed clove of garlic to the mayo for a change).

Oil-free Dressing
1 tablespoon of unsweetened concentrated apple juice
2 tablespoons of vinegar
Half a tablespoon of water
1 teaspoon of mustard
A pinch of dried tarragon
Salt and pepper

Mix the ingredients together well and combine with the salad.

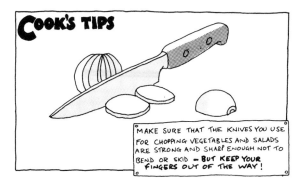

COOK'S TIPS

MAKE SURE THAT THE KNIVES YOU USE FOR CHOPPING VEGETABLES AND SALADS ARE STRONG AND SHARP ENOUGH NOT TO BEND OR SKID — BUT KEEP YOUR FINGERS OUT OF THE WAY!

SHOPPING LIST FOR WEEK ONE

For one person, assuming no goods in store

■ ■ ■ ■ ■ ■ ■ ■ ■ ■ ■ ■ ■ ■ ■ ■

FRUIT AND VEGETABLES

Various fruit:
pears, bananas, apples, oranges, etc.
6 potatoes for baking
6 oz (175g) of new potatoes
12 tomatoes
8 oz (225g) of mushrooms
2 Iceberg lettuces
1 packet of mixed salad leaves
2 cucumbers
1 head of garlic
2 small courgettes
4 small onions   Salad onions
4 runner beans   7 carrots
1 red pepper   1 green pepper
2 heads of broccoli
Small cauliflower   3 leeks
1 small packet of frozen peas
1 head of celery
Fresh basil   Fresh chives
Dried mixed herbs   2 lemons

MEAT AND FISH

1 small packet of lean back bacon
2 slices of lean ham
2 slices of lean beef
1 turkey breast, skinned and boned
8 oz (225g) of lean beef mince
8 oz (225g) lamb steak
1 salmon steak
1 chicken breast, skinned and boned
8 oz (225g) of smoked haddock or similar

DAIRY

6 medium eggs
Low-fat cheese
Low-fat cottage cheese
1 pt (60cl) of semi-skimmed milk (for cooking)
Skimmed milk (for tea and coffee)
Diet yoghurts

SUNDRIES

1 packet of high-fibre cereal (Shredded
Wheat, All-Bran, etc.)
1 loaf of whole-wheat bread
1 small jar of sugar substitute
(e.g. Candarel) if needed
1 jar of Marmite, Vegemite or low-sugar
jam for breakfast
1 small can of tuna in brine
Low-calorie mayonnaise
Oil-free dressing
1 packet of Ryvita or similar
1 jar of passata (sugar free tomato sauce)
Boil-in-the-bag brown and wild rice
Boil-in-the-bag basmati rice
3 small cans of plum tomatoes
1 jar of mixed herbs
1 small bottle of olive oil
1 packet of whole-wheat pasta
1 packet of bay leaves
Wholemeal flour   Mustard   Paprika
Cinnamon stick Cardomom pods (both optional)
Salt and pepper
Whole black peppercorns   Silver foil

Turkey Strips with Tomato and Garlic

1 turkey breast, skinned and boned
8 tablespoons of passata
3 cloves of garlic
Salt and pepper

Cut the turkey breast into strips $\frac{3}{4}$ in (2 cm) wide.

Put the passata, garlic and turkey into a small, shallow, frying-pan and cook over a low heat for about 10 to 15 minutes until the turkey is cooked through.

Serve with boil-in-the-bag mixed brown and wild rice, or with ratatouille prepared by steaming the following vegetables for 20 minutes or casseroling them for an hour with a tablespoon of olive oil: 3 sliced runner beans, 1 cubed tomato, 2 small, sliced courgettes, 1 small sliced onion, salt and pepper.

To give more flavour to the rice, add a whole cinnamon stick and two cardamom pods to the boiling water while the rice is cooking – the bag in which the rice comes is semi-permeable.

Baked Salmon Parcels

1 salmon steak
2 teaspoons of chopped fresh basil
1 sliced tomato
1 small sliced onion
Salt and pepper
Silver foil

Preheat the oven to 325°F (160°C, Gas Mark 3).

Put half the onion and half the tomato in the centre of a large piece of foil (shiny side in). Put the salmon steak on top, then top this off with the remaining tomato and onion and add the chopped basil. Season with salt and pepper.

Fold in the foil, making a tight parcel, and bake in the preheated oven for 20 to 25 minutes, until the salmon closest to the bone is cooked.

Serve with boiled new potatoes and a mixed salad of lettuce, tomato, cucumber, celery and mushrooms.

Tomato and Basil Pasta

1 cup of whole-wheat pasta
1 tablespoon of olive oil
2 small tins of plum tomatoes
3 cloves of garlic, peeled and crushed
3 fresh tomatoes, chopped
A handful of fresh basil leaves, chopped
1 tablespoon of olive oil
Salt and pepper

Put the plum tomatoes, fresh tomatoes, garlic, salt, pepper and olive oil in a saucepan and simmer gently for 45 minutes. Be careful not to let the pan get too hot or the bottom may burn. Stir frequently.

Meanwhile, cook the pasta by placing it together with the oil and some salt in a pan of fast-boiling water and cook as directed on the packet. It is ready when it is tender but not soft.

Drain the pasta and serve it with the tomato sauce and a sprinkling of freshly chopped basil.

Accompany with a mixed salad and oil-free dressing.

COOK'S TIPS

YOU CAN PREVENT PASTA FROM STICKING TOGETHER (AND STICKING TO THE PAN) BY POURING HALF A TEASPOON OF OLIVE OIL INTO THE PAN WHILST YOU ARE COOKING IT.

Grilled Lamb Steak

> 8 oz (225 g) lamb steak
> Mixed herbs
> Black pepper

Grind the black pepper or crush with the flat of a knife, and rub this and the herbs into both sides of the steak. Set the grill on high, wait for it to warm up, then grill the lamb for about 6 minutes on either side.

Accompany with boiled new potatoes and a fresh green salad with oil-free dressing.

Shepherd's Pie

> 8 oz (225 g) of lean beef mince
> 1 chopped onion
> 1 small tin of plum tomatoes
> 1 clove of garlic, peeled and crushed
> 1 carrot, peeled and diced
> Mixed herbs
> 3 large peeled potatoes
> 1 tablespoon of olive oil
> Salt and pepper

Preheat the oven to 325°F (160°C, Gas Mark 3).

Put the potatoes in a pan of cold water with a pinch of salt and boil until soft, about 20 to 25 minutes. Drain them and then mash well.

Heat the olive oil in a deep pan and lightly fry the onion and garlic. Add the mince and carrot and gently fry until the meat has lost its bright red colour and turned a dull brown. Now add the tomatoes, mixed herbs and salt and pepper, and cook over a moderate heat for about 30 minutes. Transfer to an oven-proof dish, top with the mashed potato and bake in the preheated oven for 30 minutes.

Serve with steamed mixed vegetables and passata (*not* sugar-filled tomato ketchup).

Lemon Chicken

> 1 chicken breast, skinned and boned
> 2 lemons
> 1 tablespoon of olive oil
> 1 teaspoon of paprika
> 2 tablespoons of wholemeal flour
> Salt and pepper

Preheat the oven to 325°F (180°C, Gas Mark 3).

Squeeze the juice from one and a half lemons, and slice the remaining half thinly.

Mix the flour and the paprika together and coat the chicken in it.

Heat the oil in a saucepan, then add the flour-coated chicken and brown it on all sides, being careful not to burn it. Place the chicken in a small, shallow, oven-proof dish, season with salt and pepper, pour over the lemon juice and cover the chicken with the slices of lemon. Bake uncovered for half an hour or until the chicken is cooked through.

Serve with a jacket potato with a tablespoon of cottage cheese and a green salad with oil-free dressing.

COOK'S TIPS

TAKE FROZEN FOODS OUT OF THE FREEZER AT LEAST 8 HOURS BEFORE YOU INTEND TO COOK THEM. THIS WILL ENSURE THAT THEY THAW OUT THOROUGHLY AND MAKE COOKING EASIER

4 FITNESS FUEL

EVENING MEALS FOR WEEK ONE

Easy Smoked Haddock Kedgeree

8 oz (225 g) of smoked haddock or similar
1 small, finely chopped onion lightly fried in a
tablespoon of olive oil
1 pt (60 cl) of semi-skimmed milk
1 bayleaf
2 diced tomatoes
Half a packet of boil-in-the-bag basmati rice,
cooked as per packet instructions
Salt and pepper

Put the haddock, bayleaf, some salt and pepper, and the milk into a small saucepan. Simmer the fish in the milk for 10 to 15 minutes, until the flesh is just beginning to come away from the bone. Do not let the milk boil too violently. Bin the milk, bay leaf and fish skin.

Flake the haddock and combine it with the rice, tomato and the finely chopped onion in an oven-proof dish. Season well with pepper (beware of over-salting as the fish itself is fairly salty), cover the dish with baking foil and warm through in the oven at 275°F (140°C, Gas Mark 1) for 20 minutes.

Serve with a fresh green salad with oil-free dressing.

SUGGESTED MENU FOR WEEK ONE

	Breakfast	Lunch	Supper
Monday	Hi-fibre cereal with skimmed milk, 1 slice of whole-wheat toast with Marmite or low-sugar jam, 1 piece of fruit *or* a diet yoghurt	1 boiled egg, 2 slices of whole-wheat toast, 1 piece of fruit	Turkey strips with tomato
Tuesday	Same	Whole-wheat sandwich, 1 piece of fruit	Shepherd's pie
Wednesday	Same	Tuna salad, 1 piece of fruit	Baked salmon parcels
Thursday	Same	Whole-wheat sandwich, 1 piece of fruit	Lemon chicken
Friday	Same	Jacket potato with filling and salad	Tomato and basil pasta
Saturday	Same	Whole-wheat sandwich, 1 piece of fruit	Grilled lamb steak
Sunday	Grilled breakfast, 1 piece of fruit *or* a diet yoghurt	Jacket potato with filling and salad	Smoked haddock kedgeree

Feel free to drink tea or coffee with skimmed milk and low-calorie sweeteners (if necessary) at the end of each meal. You can also have a glass of beer or wine with supper if you want.

SHOPPING LIST FOR WEEK TWO

For one person, assuming that the only goods in store are from week one

■ ■ ■ ■ ■ ■ ■ ■ ■ ■ ■ ■ ■ ■ ■ ■ ■

FRUIT AND VEGETABLES

Various fruit:
pears, bananas, apples, oranges, etc.
7 potatoes   3 tomatoes
8 oz (225g) of mushrooms
2 iceberg lettuces
1 packet of mixed salad leaves
1 cucumber   1 head of garlic
2 small courgettes
5 onions   Salad onions
5 carrots
1 red pepper   1 green pepper
Brussels sprouts
1 parsnip   1 turnip   1 leek
1 head of celery   Broccoli
1 small cauliflower
Small piece of fresh ginger
Fresh basil
Fresh rosemary, or dried
Parsley
1 small packet of frozen peas

MEAT AND FISH

1 packet of lean back bacon
6 slices of lean ham
6 slices of lean beef
8 oz (225g) of lean beef mince
1 lb (450g) of pork tenderloin
2 chicken portions
1 lb (450g) of lean braising steak
2 tubs of fresh beef stock,
or low-salt beef stock cubes

DAIRY

Low-fat hard cheese
Low-fat cottage cheese
Skimmed milk (for tea and coffee)
Diet yoghurts

SUNDRIES

1 packet of high-fibre cereal (Shredded
Wheat, All-Bran, etc.)
1 loaf of whole-wheat bread
2 small cans of tuna in brine
1 small can of plum tomatoes
Boil-in-the-bag brown rice
1 packet of whole-wheat spaghetti
1 jar of passata
Crusty brown rolls
Low salt vegetable or chicken stock cubes
Wholemeal plain flour
Half a bottle of red wine
1 small can of unsweetened pineapple chunks
1 pizza base

EVENING MEALS FOR WEEK TWO

Vegetable and Bacon Soup

1 small onion
2 small carrots
1 parsnip
1 turnip
1 potato
1 leek
2 sticks of celery
1 sprig of parsley
2 rashers of lean back bacon, chopped
1 low-salt vegetable or chicken stock cube
1 tablespoon of olive oil
Salt and pepper
Crusty brown rolls

Wash, peel and chop the vegetables.

Heat the oil in a large pan and lightly fry the onion, being careful not to burn it. Add the remaining vegetables and the bacon, then cook over a gentle heat for 5 to 10 minutes until the vegetables start to soften. Add the stock cube, cover the vegetables with water and season with salt and pepper.

Simmer the soup gently for about 45 minutes. At this stage you can liquidize the soup or just serve it as it is with crusty brown rolls warmed in the oven.

Kebabs

1 chicken breast, skinned and boned, or 8 oz (225 g) of pork tenderloin
6 mushrooms
Half a red pepper
Half a green pepper
2 small onions, quartered
2 small courgettes, sliced thickly
1 tablespoon of olive oil
Salt and pepper

Chop the meat and peppers into chunks about 1 in (2.5 cm) square and thread them and the other ingredients on to long skewers, alternating the colours. Season them with salt and pepper and brush all over with olive oil.

Grill under a moderate heat or cook on a barbecue.

Serve on a bed of cooked, cold brown rice with a green salad.

Pork with Pineapple and Ginger

8 oz (225 g) of pork tenderloin, cubed
1 small can of pineapple pieces, *unsweetened*
1 small piece of fresh ginger, peeled and chopped
1 tablespoon of olive oil
Salt and pepper

Heat the oil in a large frying-pan. Gently add the ginger and pork and stir frequently to prevent the meat sticking. When the pork is almost cooked (about 10 to 15 minutes), add the pineapple and heat through.

Serve immediately with boil-in-the-bag brown rice and a mixed salad.

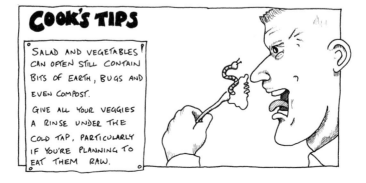

COOK'S TIPS

SALAD AND VEGETABLES CAN OFTEN STILL CONTAIN BITS OF EARTH, BUGS AND EVEN COMPOST.

GIVE ALL YOUR VEGGIES A RINSE UNDER THE COLD TAP, PARTICULARLY IF YOU'RE PLANNING TO EAT THEM RAW.

EVENING MEALS FOR WEEK TWO

Spaghetti Bolognese

Use the same mince recipe as for shepherd's pie but add to whole-wheat spaghetti. The pasta should be cooked with some salt and a tablespoon of olive oil in fast-boiling water as per the instructions on the packet. Serve it when it is tender but not soft, and accompany with a large salad of your choice.

Beef Stew with Mushrooms and Wine

1 lb (450 g) of lean stewing or braising steak, cubed
1 onion, chopped
2 carrots, peeled and sliced
2 tablespoons of flour
2 tablespoons of olive oil
2 tubs of fresh beef stock or $1\frac{1}{2}$ pt (90 cl) made from cubes
Mixed herbs
8 mushrooms, sliced
Glass of red wine
1 bay leaf
Salt and pepper

Preheat the oven to 300°F (150°C, Gas Mark 2).

Coat the beef in the flour, then heat the oil in a frying-pan and quickly fry the meat to give a good colour on all sides. Be careful not to burn it. Place all the ingredients together with the meat in a casserole dish and pour on the stock. Cover and cook slowly in the oven for about 2 hours, or until the meat is tender.

Serve with steamed peas and carrots and a jacket potato.

This is enough for *two* meals.

Pizza

1 ready-to-use pizza base
2 tablespoons of passata
2 teaspoons of chopped fresh basil
2 rashers of lean back bacon, grilled then chopped
1 sliced tomato
2 tablespoons of grated low-fat cheese
Salt and pepper

Preheat the oven to 350°F (180°C, Gas Mark 4).

Spread the passata evenly on the pizza base, then arrange the tomato and bacon on the top. Sprinkle the cheese and basil over it and add salt and pepper. Vegetables such as onion or mushrooms could also be added to the topping.

Bake in the oven for about 20 minutes and serve with a green salad.

Roast Chicken with Rosemary

1 skinless chicken quarter
1 sprig of chopped fresh rosemary (or 1 teaspoon of dried)
1 teaspoon of olive oil
Salt and pepper

Preheat the oven to 350°F (180°C, Gas Mark 4).

Rub the olive oil into the chicken quarter and sprinkle rosemary over the top. Season with salt and pepper, then place in a roasting tray in the oven and bake until cooked through, about 25 to 30 minutes.

Serve with steamed Brussels sprouts and a jacket potato.

COOK'S TIPS

WHEN YOU COOK CHICKEN, ENSURE THAT IT IS COOKED RIGHT THROUGH. IF IT IS AT ALL PINK OR BLOODY, PUT IT BACK ON TO COOK. THIS WILL PROTECT YOU AGAINST STOMACH UPSETS.

4 FITNESS FUEL

EVENING MEALS FOR WEEK TWO

SUGGESTED MENU FOR WEEK TWO

	Breakfast	Lunch	Supper
Monday	Hi-fibre cereal with skimmed milk, I slice of whole-wheat toast with Marmite or low-sugar jam, I piece of fruit *or* a diet yoghurt	I boiled egg, 2 slices of whole-wheat toast, I piece of fruit	Roast chicken with rosemary
Tuesday	Same	Whole-wheat sandwich, I piece of fruit	Spaghetti bolognese
Wednesday	Same	Tuna salad, I piece of fruit	Pork with pineapple and ginger
Thursday	Same	Whole-wheat sandwich, I piece of fruit	Pizza with salad
Friday	Same	Jacket potato with filling and salad	Vegetable and bacon soup
Saturday	Same	Whole-wheat sandwich, I piece of fruit	Kebabs
Sunday	Grilled breakfast, I piece of fruit *or* a diet yoghurt	Jacket potato with filling and salad	Beef stew with mushrooms and wine

Feel free to drink tea or coffee with skimmed milk and low-calorie sweeteners (if necessary) at the end of each meal. You can also have a glass of beer or wine with supper if you want.

SPECIAL FOODS AND SUPPLEMENTS

In a lot of health food and specialist sports stores, you will see shelves weighed down with various types of food supplements, drinks and pills aimed at sportsmen and women, body-builders and so on. Most of these promise some vague improvement in performance to the person who is prepared to shell out the high prices that are demanded of them. With a few exceptions, these claims are bogus or nearly so, because you can obtain exactly the same benefits by eating foods containing the same substances at a much lower cost and with much better taste.

Food and fluid supplements are useful in certain circumstances, however, as follows:

Fluid Replacement Drinks

There are an increasing number of special drinks on the market that are designed to help replace the water and minerals that you lose during exercise. Among the better known brands are Gatorade, Isostar, Lucozade Sport and Dexters. These taste pretty good and, if they do actually replace fluid more quickly than drinking straight water, may be of some benefit. Even so, they are expensive and the benefits are marginal – I only drink them because I like the taste! Some people drink Dioralyte, which is a preparation designed for patients suffering dehydration as a consequence of diarrhoea. This is not recommended, as Dioralyte is a medicine and should only be used under trained medical supervision.

Vitamin Supplements

You can buy all kinds of vitamin supplements from pharmacies, health-food stores and supermarkets, but if you eat a properly balanced diet there is no need to. I would consider taking some multivitamin pills if I was going to be away from home for a while, and thus not sure whether I would be eating properly, but not otherwise. The quantities of vitamins that your body needs are fairly small and you will get all of them from the diet described in this chapter. Excess vitamins are, generally speaking, excreted in your urine – almost literally pouring your money down the drain!

Protein Supplements

You are not likely to require protein supplements for the same reason that you don't need vitamin supplements – you will get more than enough from a healthy, balanced diet. Excess protein goes the same way that excess vitamins do – down the drain. It is possible that protein supplements help body-builders (though not as much as a couple of years in psychoanalysis would), but even they should be able to get all they need from protein-rich foods.

Even if supplements do work, they will only do so in conjunction with exercise. Many people have abused anabolic steroids in the mistaken belief that they will build muscles without effort, but this is not the case – and the same is true for 'legal' supplements. If food supplements work at all, it is simply by giving a slight edge over those who are training as hard but without the supplement.

CHAPTER 5
THE FIGHTING FIT
TRAINING
PROGRAMMES

PUTTING IT TOGETHER

IT IS TIME to put together all the information from the last four chapters and combine it into training programmes. There are three in this chapter, all designed for people who don't currently take much exercise but want to start getting fit, and they should all be combined with the sort of food described in Chapter 4.

The Desk Driver's programme takes up the least time and involves the least effort. It is designed on the principle that any exercise is better than none, but it will have a very noticeable effect on your general fitness. Unless you want to play sport at the weekend, you do not need any special equipment other than the basic training gear described in Chapter 1, and you don't need to go to a gym or sports centre (unless you want to!).

The Semi-Pro programme is for people who want to improve their fitness significantly, but who don't have the time or need to scale the heights of the full Fighting Fit programme. To complete the Semi-Pro programme, you need to have access to a swimming pool and, preferably, a sports centre.

The Fighting Fit programme will take you to a very high level of physical fitness. It requires determination and dedication to see it through, but by the end you will be ready to conquer the world (well, nearly). To complete the Fighting Fit programme, you will need to have access to a gym and a swimming pool and be prepared to visit them several times each week. As the programme takes four months to complete, you should also be prepared to suffer some wear and tear on both your body and your equipment.

How the Programmes Work

The Fighting Fit programmes are designed to get you to the level of fitness you want in the shortest possible time, with the least amount of physical stress. They start gently enough and progress in a way that will accustom you to taking a lot of exercise in small, easily manageable doses. They will also accommodate any sporting activity that you normally take part in. If you play soccer, rugby, tennis, squash or any other high-activity sport, you can substitute it for any training session in the programme and then continue as normal the next day. Be warned however: you don't get fit overnight. No diet or fitness programme works unless you stick with it, and you *must* discipline yourself. Despite that, the Fighting Fit programmes are easy to follow because the high level of activity means that you need to worry much less about your food intake. It won't matter if you indulge in an occasional blow-out and you can certainly have a few beers every now and again.

What About Interruptions?

Don't worry if you miss a day now and then – enjoy the rest and console yourself with the thought that your body is being given an unexpected day off. Similarly, if you find the training load becoming too much, take an extra day off to recover – you've earned it and you will find it easier to get back into the swing after a rest. But if you get an injury or become ill, or you are forced to stop training for more than five days for some other reason, you will have to drop back at least a week in the programme (and probably more for illness or injury). Don't get downhearted, though. The next chapter explains how to deal with injury in far more detail, but the baseline is that it is foolish to attempt to train through illnesses or injuries because, nine times out of ten, you will only make them worse, possibly doing yourself serious and permanent damage in the process. Accept the setback and resolve to fight on – remember, nobody ever said it was going to be easy!

If you have any doubts about your ability to cope with the exercise programmes described in this chapter, check first with your doctor (and remember to take this book with you so that he or she knows what you're talking about!).

IT IS ALL TOO EASY to become hung up on fitness and dieting – just look at the number of people who develop eating disorders like anorexia or bulimia. Much of this has been aided by the 'health' industry, which continues to advertise spurious dieting aids and fitness books which promise quick fixes. The fact is that they don't work, but scare tactics are causing more and more people to try them. There is no point in following some trendy new health fad if you're going to turn into a psychotic weirdo as a result – so here are a few factors to think about before you turn down the second helping of that delicious pudding and reach for the distilled water.

Food

The quantity of exercise you take on the Fighting Fit programmes will markedly raise the amount of food that you can eat without getting fat. If you graduate to the most demanding programmes, you should aim to eat about 2,000 calories a day of the sort of foods described in Chapter 4 – and if someone invites you out for a meal, or you fancy going out yourself, you're not going to turn into the Michelin man. Provided you aren't pigging out every other night, the odd big meal will do you no harm at all.

Drink

If you want a beer or a glass of wine, have one. Treat alcohol as food – lager is about 200 calories per pint, for example. But remember: if you're getting loaded on a regular basis, you've got a problem which you need to get sorted out. A fit person will be able to handle a moderate booze-up occasionally, but you have to be sensible about it. Incidentally, don't take exercise when you're very hung-over – the chances are that you will be dehydrated which could lead to serious heat injuries. Stay in bed and promise yourself that you will never, ever do it again.

Smoking

Inevitably some smokers will try to follow the programmes, and some will be able to handle them with ease. Think, as you're coughing your guts up after the session, how much easier it would be if you didn't smoke. You may know some smart-arse Mister Fitty who piles down 40 a day and can still run a 4-minute mile, but he's probably lying. Anyway, think how much faster he could go if he didn't smoke.

And Finally ...

Don't become a PT hermit. Exercise shouldn't normally take up more than an hour or so per day, including changing and showering time, so don't let it stop you from doing other things that you enjoy. After a while, you will find that you have more energy for things like playing with the kids, or even sex, so take advantage of it. Good health and fitness should be a part of your life, but try not to let it rule your life.

STAYING SHARP

BY NOW YOU will have realized that one of the hardest parts of any fitness programme or diet is actually staying with it. As the nights draw in and the weather gets bad, it can be all too easy to start skipping training much too often. If you do this, you won't be able to stick with the programme, you won't make the gains that you should be making and you may lose the will to continue – it can happen to anyone. So how to avoid this? Quite easily, in fact, and outlined below are some basic techniques which can help you beat the poor-motivation blues.

Goal Setting

The most basic motivating technique is goal setting. The reason that anyone starts a fitness programme or diet is to get fitter or lose weight. Unfortunately, both of these things take time – you cannot go from running an 8-minute mile to running a 4-minute mile overnight, just as you can't lose 20 lb in a week. The trick is to set yourself intermediate and realistic goals.

Suppose that you are 20 lb overweight at the start of the Fighting Fit programme. The Fighting Fit programme lasts for 16 weeks, during which you are going to take a lot of exercise and eat sensibly (without starving yourself). Sixteen weeks is a long time and, while you know that the weight is falling off you, 20 lb is a fair bit to lose. At times you will be asking yourself 'Is it worth it?' because the gains that you are achieving don't seem too special against the overall target that you've set. The answer is to set yourself a realistic weekly target of losing 1 lb – which is not at all difficult and represents a much more immediate achievement.

When you get up on the first day of the programme, empty your bowels, weigh yourself and make a note of the result. Do the same thing at the same time every week and you will see how much progress you are making. After you've been doing this for a month, assess your level of success – you may be able to shift your target to losing 2 lb a week, or you may find that you're not shedding weight quickly enough and need to think about your food intake. (Unless you're pigging out on every available goodie, you should be able to lose 2 lb a week with ease.)

You can do much the same thing for running, swimming and lifting weights. Note the time it takes to run or swim a set distance, remember the weight with

which you can comfortably perform 12 reps, and set a target to beat each week. It is the same as the old proverb: 'Look after the pennies and the pounds will look after themselves.' What's more, it works.

Mental Visualization

The second technique is complementary to the first. All that visualization requires you to do is fantasize. When you are out running, or in the pool, or in the gym, imagine how you are going to look with no excess fat, more muscular definition and the improved posture and body shape that accompanies real fitness – not bad at all, huh? Forget the pain, because when you've finished the programme you really are going to look like that! Each time you push a weight in the bench press, think about your pectorals getting larger and stronger; each mile you run, think how your heart and lungs are getting more powerful, more efficient. Look at the people who aren't training with you and remember how much they are going to want to be like you when you achieve your ultimate goal.

Having completed one or more of the programmes and achieved an improved level of physical fitness, it is essential that you don't give in to the temptation to rest on your laurels and slide back into your old ways. With your new-found fitness, you will have a great deal more energy and ability to get things done. You will also have accustomed your body to taking a lot of exercise. But there's no point in getting stale either – chances are that you will become bored with an endless round of gym workouts, running and swimming.

The solution is to look around for alternatives. With the full Fighting Fit programme, for example, you will have achieved a level of all-round fitness that will enable you to take up a new sport or activity with ease – ease because you won't have to worry too much about supplementary fitness training. So look around; you might decide that you've always wanted to play squash, or go scuba diving, or windsurfing, or climbing – all of these are now possible because you are fit.

To stay sharp, all you have to do is maintain a consistent level of activity. Decide that you are going to exercise for six days every week and stick to that. It doesn't matter what you do provided that you are getting your heart rate into the training range for at least three of the sessions for at least 30 minutes – but two runs and a game of squash will see to that. Enjoy yourself by playing some football or rugby, or go for a swim, for the other sessions – just don't get bored. And if you feel that your fitness is slipping, try doing the last month of the programme over again. Remember: by getting yourself Fighting Fit, you've won the hardest battle of all – against yourself!

THE DESK DRIVER'S PROGRAMME

IF YOU REALLY can't spare more than half an hour a day, or you haven't tried to take exercise since you hung up your short trousers for the last time, then this is the programme for you. The aim is to get you taking 20 minutes of exercise every day but imposing the minimum of physical strain. You must discipline yourself to take the exercise, but you should find that you start to feel much brighter and more perky after a few weeks and the benefits will stand for themselves. When you have completed the Desk Driver's programme, you'll be ready to graduate to the next one, the Semi-Pro.

Jogging

Jogging is gentle running at a pace that you feel comfortable with. When you first start, don't even think about going for longer than 20 minutes and try to find a circuit of about $2-2\frac{1}{2}$ miles (3–4 km) that starts and finishes at your home so you will always be within easy walking distance. If you have to stop and walk, don't worry – it happens to all of us!

Sport

If you don't play any sport then think about taking one up; alternatively, you could try an exercise class at your local gymnasium or sports centre. If you do play sport, take it easy! Unless you have plenty of time in which to train during the week, you could do yourself an injury trying to emulate Maradona or Will Carling. Less intense sports (like cricket or sailing) won't do you any harm, but don't kid yourself that a few frames of snooker or a game of darts are going to get you fit.

The Home Workout

Detailed descriptions of these exercises are in Chapter 2, but rest assured that you don't need any special gear for them and you can do them all in your living-room. Start off with the instructions in the following list, but as you get fitter you should be able to perform more repetitions in each set.

HOME HEARTWARMER		
1	Warm-Up	3 minutes. See Chapter 2.
2	Press-Ups	20 reps then 1 minute rest.
3	Crunches	20 reps then 30 seconds rest.
4	Press-Ups	20 reps then 30 seconds rest.
5	Leg Raises	25 reps then 30 seconds rest.
6	Press-Ups	20 reps then 30 seconds rest.
7	V-Crunches	20 reps then 30 seconds rest.
8	Press-Ups	20 reps then 30 seconds rest.
9	Hyperextensions	20 reps then 30 seconds rest.
10	Tricep Dips	20 reps then 30 seconds rest (use a sofa to support your hands and a stool or chair to support your feet).
11	Crossover Crunches	20 reps then 30 seconds rest.
12	Tricep Dips	20 reps then 30 seconds rest.
13	Leg Raises	25 reps then stretch off to cool down.

When you've done that, warm down and take a hot bath or shower.

THE DESK DRIVER'S PROGRAMME

DAY	WEEK 1	2	3	4
Monday	Jog – 20 mins	Home workout – 20 mins	Jog – 20 mins	Home workout – 20 mins
Tuesday	Home workout – 20 mins	Jog – 20 mins	Home workout – 20 mins	Jog – 20 mins
Wednesday	Jog – 20 mins	Home workout – 20 mins	Jog – 20 mins	Home workout – 20 mins
Thursday	Home workout – 20 mins	Jog – 20 mins	Home workout – 20 mins	Jog – 20 mins
Friday	Day off	Day off	Day off	Day off
Saturday	Sport – up to 90 mins	Sport – up to 90 mins	Sport – up to 90 mins	Sport – up to 90 mins
Sunday	Swim or jog – 20 mins	Swim or jog – 20 mins	Swim or jog – 20 mins	Swim or jog – 20 mins

THE SEMI-PRO PROGRAMME

THE SEMI-PRO PROGRAMME is designed for the person who is keen to attain a reasonable level of fitness but doesn't have the time available to follow the full Fighting Fit programme. It is a progressive programme which builds up over four weeks to a level at which you will be increasing your cardio-vascular fitness and toning your muscles without having to exercise for more than 30 minutes each day (except on sport days). The completion of this programme will set you up nicely for the start of the full Fighting Fit programme.

Swimming

Your best bet with swimming is to start off by simply swimming lengths of the pool at a pace that you feel comfortable with, using either the breast-stroke or front crawl. As your fitness increases, consider using the swimming workouts described in Chapter 2. Don't spend too long at the end of the pool 'resting' after each length!

Sport

After four weeks of the Semi-Pro programme, you will be fit enough to make a good showing in most sports.

In fact, if you remember to warm up properly, there's no reason why you shouldn't make a balls-out effort every time you play. If you play sport for a team, consider attending a mid-week training session and substitute that for one of the workouts in the programme.

Days Off

Friday is marked as the day off to give you a chance to wind down at the end of the week and relax. If there is a more convenient day to take off, then simply shunt the programme around to accommodate it.

Missing Days

Don't worry if you miss a day on the Semi-Pro programme – just continue as if you'd done it anyway. If you miss a week or more then you should seriously think about starting again. Go for a couple of jogs and a swim or two and listen to what your body is telling you – but don't give up!

THE SEMI-PRO PROGRAMME

DAY	WEEK 1	2	3	4
Monday	Jog – 20 mins	Jog – 25 mins	Jog – 30 mins	Jog – 30 mins
Tuesday	Swim – 20 mins	Swim – 20 mins or an exercise class	Swim – 20 mins or an exercise class	Swim – 30 mins or an exercise class
Wednesday	Jog – 20 mins	Jog – 30 mins	Jog – 30 mins	Jog – 30 mins
Thursday	Swim – 20 mins	Swim – 20 mins	Swim – 30 mins or an exercise class	Swim – 30 mins or multigym circuit – 30 mins
Friday	Day off	Day off	Day off	Day off
Saturday	Sport – 90 mins	Sport – 90 mins	Sport – 90 mins	Sport – 90 mins
Sunday	Swim – 30 mins	Swim – 30 mins	Swim – 30 mins	Swim – 30 mins

THE FIGHTING FIT PROGRAMME

DAY	WEEK 1	WEEK 2	WEEK 3	WEEK 4
Monday	Easy run – 30 mins	Easy run – 30 mins	Easy run – 30 mins	Easy run – 30 mins
Tuesday	Swim – 30 mins	Swim – 30 mins – or super circuit	Swim – 30 mins – or super circuit	Swim – 30 mins – or super circuit
Wednesday	Easy run – 45 mins – or sport for 90 mins	Easy run – 45 mins – or sport for 90 mins	Basic run – 45 mins – or sport for 90 mins	Basic run – 45 mins – or sport for 90 mins
Thursday	Swim – 30 mins continuous or pyramids	Swim – 30 mins – or super circuit	Multigym circuit – 3 complete sets	Multigym circuit – 3 complete sets
Friday	Easy run – 30 mins	Basic run – 45 mins	Basic run – 45 mins	Basic run – 45 mins
Saturday	Day off	Day off	Swim – 30 mins	Swim – 30 mins
Sunday	Long easy run – 1 hour	Long easy run – 1 hour	Long easy run – 1 hour	Long easy run – 1 hour

What to Expect

The Fighting Fit programme is a 16-week training course for those who are seriously committed to getting fit. It is progressive and begins reasonably gently, so you can choose either to start from scratch or do the Desk Driver's and Semi-Pro programmes first to get used to taking exercise. Make no mistake, the Fighting Fit programme requires a lot of effort, commitment and self-discipline but the benefits for those who stick with it will be enormous. Sports you can play to vary the routine include soccer, rugby, tennis and squash.

The First Month

It is going to take you a while to accustom yourself to the exercise and it may hurt a little, but you know it's worth it. Your first month on the Fighting Fit programme is an introduction to regular physical training, but by the end of the second week you will really notice the difference. The most important thing is to take the exercises gently – an 'easy run' means just that. If you are training with a partner, make sure that he or she is either of the same standard as you or doesn't mind taking it easy until you catch up.

THE FIGHTING FIT PROGRAMME

DAY	WEEK 5	WEEK 6	WEEK 7	WEEK 8
Monday	Basic run – 45 mins	Fast run – 30 mins	Fartlek workout – 45 mins	Fast run – 30 mins
Tuesday	Swim – 30 mins – or super circuit	Swim – 30 mins – or super circuit	Swim – 30 mins – or super circuit	Swim – 30 mins – or super circuit
Wednesday	Basic run – 45 mins – or sport for 90 mins	Basic run – 45 mins – or sport for 90 mins	Basic run – 45 mins – or sport for 90 mins	Basic run – 45 mins – or sport for 90 mins
Thursday	Multigym circuit – 3 complete sets	Multigym circuit – 3 complete sets	Multigym circuit – 3 complete sets	Multigym circuit – 3 complete sets
Friday	Basic run – 45 mins	Basic run – 45 mins	Fast run – 30 mins	Fartlek workout – 45 mins
Saturday	Swim – 30 mins or day off	Swim – 30 mins or day off	Swim – 30 mins or day off	Swim – 30 mins or day off
Sunday	Long easy run – 1 hour	Long easy run – 1 hour	Long easy run – 1 hour 15 mins	Long easy run – 1 hour 15 mins

The Second Month

By now the difference in your fitness will be visible to everyone. You will be leaner, and your body will be becoming much more 'defined' as you build up muscles in the pool and the gym. The second month sees the start of speed training for your legs, and by the end of the eighth week your running times will have increased enough for you to start looking for longer routes for your runs (you should be running between 20 and 25 miles, or 32–40 km, a week by now). The chances are that you will also be needing more sleep – don't fight this, as you need it to recover from the increased workload. You should also be careful to ensure that you are drinking enough water to avoid dehydration (your urine should be clear – the darker it gets, the more dehydrated you are).

THE FIGHTING FIT PROGRAMME

DAY	WEEK 9	10	11	12
Monday	Fartlek workout – 45 mins	Interval workout – 4 × 400 metres	Fast run – 30 mins	Fartlek workout – 45 mins
Tuesday	1 Swim – 30 mins – or super circuit 2 Easy run – 30 mins (optional)	Swim – 30 mins – or super circuit	Swim – 30 mins – or super circuit	1 Swim – 30 mins – or super circuit 2 Easy run – 30 mins (optional)
Wednesday	Basic run – 45 mins – or sport for 90 mins	Basic run – 45 mins – or sport for 90 mins	Basic run – 45 mins – or sport for 90 mins	Basic run – 45 mins – or sport for 90 mins
Thursday	Multigym circuit – 3 complete sets	1 Multigym circuit – 3 complete sets 2 Easy run – 30 mins	1 Multigym circuit – 3 complete sets 2 Easy run – 30 mins	1 Multigym circuit – 3 complete sets 2 Easy run – 30 mins
Friday	Basic run – 45 mins	Basic run – 45 mins	Basic run – 45 mins	Basic run – 45 mins
Saturday	Swim – 30 mins – or day off	Swim or cycle – 30 mins – or day off	Day off	Day off
Sunday	Long easy run – 1 hour 15 mins	Long easy run – 1 hour 15 mins	Long easy run – 1 hour 15 mins	Long easy run – 1 hour 15 mins

The Third Month

At the start of the third month, we begin to try out two training sessions a day. Take this *very* easy at first because it may turn out to be too much for you at this stage – and, if possible, spread the exercises so that you do one set in the morning and one in the evening. By now you should be running 25–30 miles (40–48 km) per week.

THE FIGHTING FIT PROGRAMME

DAY	WEEK 13	14	15	16
Monday	Interval workout – 8 × 400 metres	Fast run – 30 mins	Fartlek workout – 45 mins	Interval workout – 4 × 800 metres
Tuesday	1 Swim – 30 mins – or super circuit 2 Easy run – 30 mins	1 Swim – 30 mins – or super circuit 2 Easy run – 30 mins	1 Swim – 30 mins – or super circuit 2 Easy run – 30 mins	1 Swim – 30 mins – or super circuit 2 Easy run – 30 mins
Wednesday	Basic run – 45 mins – or sport for 90 mins	Basic run – 45 mins – or sport for 90 mins	Basic run – 45 mins – or sport for 90 mins	Basic run – 45 mins – or sport for 90 mins
Thursday	1 Multigym circuit – 3 complete sets 2 Easy run – 30 mins	1 Multigym circuit – 3 complete sets 2 Easy run – 30 mins	1 Multigym circuit – 3 complete sets 2 Easy run – 30 mins	1 Multigym circuit – 3 complete sets 2 Easy run – 30 mins
Friday	Basic run – 45 mins	Basic run – 45 mins	1 Swim – 30 mins 2 Basic run – 45 mins	1 Swim – 30 mins 2 Basic run – 45 mins
Saturday	Day off	Day off	Day off	Day off
Sunday	Easy run – 1 hour 15 mins	Easy run – 1 hour 15 mins	Easy run – 1 hour 15 mins	Easy run – 1 hour 30 mins

The Fourth Month

The fourth month of the Fighting Fit programme is designed to bring you to a plateau of all-round fitness which combines a high level of cardio-vascular endurance with a sensible degree of upper-body strength. All of the 'two exercise' days should be treated with a certain amount of caution – there will certainly be times when you don't feel up to a second workout and it may be sensible to back off and leave the second exercise out altogether.

CHAPTER 6
INJURIES

INJURIES WHICH INTERFERE with your ability to take exercise can occur at almost any time. There are many reasons, although most of those which I've suffered have been caused by two factors: not warming up properly before starting exercise, and doing the exercise wrongly. The human body is a remarkably complicated piece of equipment with an amazing ability to repair itself, but pain is its signal that something is going wrong.

As you become accustomed to taking regular exercise, you will become more able to judge when pain is signalling a minor fault or when there is a more serious problem. At the start of your exercise programme, however, you must listen to your body very carefully. You must make it an absolute rule that if you are suffering from anything more than the most minor discomfort you should stop what you are doing at once. You ignore pain at your peril – it is quite possible that by disregarding a niggling injury you will create a problem that will dog you for years.

Rules for Injuries

If you find yourself suffering from any of the following symptoms during exercise, you should seek *immediate* medical attention:

> Severe chest or abdominal pains
> Severe headache
> Dizziness

You should also strongly consider seeking medical attention for either of the following:

> Nausea and vomiting
> Severe pains in the limbs and joints

Even if you decide that your injury or symptoms do not warrant immediate medical help, you should stop exercising immediately and rest whichever bit of you is causing the trouble.

Training Through Injuries

Getting an injury in the middle of a training programme can be a remarkably dispiriting event. For many people, it will signal a miserable return to their bad old habits of lethargic inactivity – but this needn't be so. If you have an ankle injury caused by running, for example, it may well be possible for you to substitute cycling or swimming minute for minute and thus not lose any cardio-vascular conditioning at all. This goes for many other injuries and alternatives as well – there is almost certainly an exercise that you will be able to do without interfering with the healing process. Accept that you will have a little catching up to do when your injury has healed, but enjoy the fact that it will be a lot less than you might have had to do if you had just lazed around. Enjoy the change in routine – you may discover a new sporting enthusiasm!

You can harden the skin of your feet to avoid blisters by rubbing them with surgical spirit every day, but the best way to avoid them is by having properly broken-in, well-fitting shoes and boots. Treat walking boots with dubbin, saddle soap or neat's-foot oil to soften the leather and wear them around your home and for short walks before you try any long distances in them.

6 INJURIES

COMMON INJURIES AND THEIR TREATMENTS

THESE ARE THE common bugbears that you may encounter when taking exercise. Aside from treating niggling ailments such as blisters and abrasions – which can be very painful at the time – do not try to be your own doctor. If you have injured yourself or are feeling unwell as a result of taking exercise, seek proper medical advice.

Blisters

Blisters are the body's defence mechanism against very high temperatures. The blisters that you get on your feet during exercise are the result of friction, and their purpose is to cushion that area against further injury. That's fine, except they bloody hurt! Opinion is divided as to whether you should empty the fluid out of blisters or not. If they are small (smaller than your index finger's nail, for example), it is probably best to cover them with a padded sticking-plaster and leave them. Larger than that and you should consider bursting them. The danger with this is infection – it is vital that you don't introduce any germs into the blister when you are fiddling with it and you must be sure to sterilize the surface of the blister and the area around it, your hands and whatever you are going to burst the blister with (a pin is the best bet). This is done by liberally dousing them all with surgical spirit or an antiseptic liquid. When everything is thoroughly sterile, make two holes in the surface of the blister and allow all of the fluid to come out before, again, soaking the area in surgical spirit (which will sting mightily) and covering with sticking-plaster.

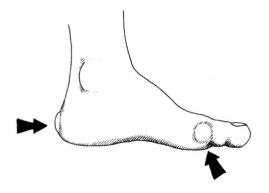

You can try to prevent blisters altogether through various means, which include taping blister-prone areas of your feet, smearing petroleum jelly on your feet and between your toes, and even soaking your socks in olive oil.

Black Toenails

Black toenails indicate bleeding and bruising beneath the nail and in extreme cases they can become horribly infected. There are two basic causes: allowing the toenails to grow too long, and exercising in poorly fitting shoes. Cutting your toenails is cheaper so try that first, but if it doesn't work then you may have to buy a new pair of shoes.

Jogger's Nipple

Jogger's nipple is an excruciatingly painful condition caused by the chafing of running vests and shirts against the nipples. As with blisters, you can attempt to prevent this by putting petroleum jelly on the nipples or by taping over them (hairy-chested men beware!).

Groin Chafing

Chafing between the legs at the groin is often suffered by those who run with their legs fairly close together. As with jogger's nipple, it can be excruciatingly painful although it isn't particularly serious. The only preventive that I have found to work 100 per cent of the time is to smear copious quantities of petroleum jelly on the afflicted area.

Stress Injuries

People who take a lot of exercise can suffer from a number of different stress injuries, most of which require the same treatment – rest. Some of the most common include:

Shin Splints
Pain and soreness around the shins is known as 'shin splints'. It can be caused by a number of factors, including inadequate warming-up, running on hard or

COMMON INJURIES AND THEIR TREATMENTS

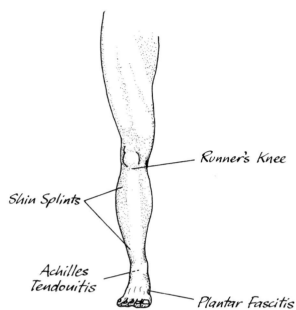

Runner's Knee

Shin Splints

Achilles Tendonitis

Plantar Fascitis

you should avoid too much sprinting and running on hilly ground.

Achilles Tendonitis
Pain in the Achilles tendon (at the back of the heel) is extremely common among runners. It can be caused by pressure from ill-fitting shoes and by excessive stretching when improperly warmed up. A good preventive is to do frequent but gentle Achilles stretches.

Plantar Fascitis
This is a very painful inflammation of the connective tissue on the sole of the foot. It can be prevented by not running on hard surfaces and by performing frequent calf stretches.

A good treatment for easing the pain from all of these injuries is known by the acronym RICE – Rest, Ice, Compression and Elevation. You need a bag of ice, wrapped in a cloth or tea-towel, and a place where you can sit or lie comfortably for 20 minutes with your injured part elevated above your heart. All you have to do is apply the ice, quite firmly, to the injured part while holding it above the level of the heart. The ice should be wrapped in a cloth to prevent 'ice burns' on the skin. This simple process eases inflammation dramatically and it can be further improved by taking aspirin or another mild painkiller.

uneven surfaces and running too fast. The problem will quickly disappear if correctly treated, but when ignored it can lead to stress fractures in the lower leg.

Runner's Knee
This is characterized by pain around or under the knee and it is caused by improper tracking of the kneecap. A good preventive measure is to build up the strength of your quadriceps muscles by cycling, but otherwise

COMMON INJURIES AND THEIR TREATMENTS

Temperature Extremes

Heat Exhaustion

Exercising in really hot weather can be bad news – it is all too easy to move through dehydration into heat exhaustion, heat stroke and death. Any of these symptoms means trouble: dizziness, headache, disorientation, nausea, decrease in sweating, and cold, clammy skin. If you notice these symptoms in yourself, or in someone you are training with, stop exercising immediately, get into shade, drink water and pour it over yourself, and seek immediate medical attention. The symptoms are normally preceded by profuse sweating and a feeling of weakness and fatigue which should lead most sensible people to abandon exercise immediately.

In this case prevention is far better than cure, so bear a few things in mind. The most important is to avoid exercising in conditions where heat will be a problem. In the tropics, for example, don't exercise during the middle of the day when the sun is hottest, use the early morning instead. Always ensure that you have plenty of (non-alcoholic) liquid to drink before, during and after any exercise you take in hot conditions, and always acclimatize slowly to heat. It is a matter of common sense – 'A man's gotta know his limitations', as Clint Eastwood once said.

Hypothermia

Hypothermia is a condition caused by a drop in the core temperature of the human body which leads to unconsciousness, cardiac and respiratory failure and death. While the condition is not likely to be a problem in most temperate climates (because it is unlikely to get cold enough to fell someone out on a 45-minute run), it is a very real danger if you are training out in the hills, or even just hiking.

Apart from low temperatures, factors which contribute to the onset of hypothermia include high winds (the wind chill factor), wetness and physical exhaustion. The symptoms are, at first, simple coldness and shivering but these then progress towards the following:

Irrational, and possibly violent, behaviour

Physical and mental lethargy

Loss of muscular co-ordination

Abnormality or failure of vision

Eventually, as the condition worsens, the sufferer slides into coma and then dies. First aid for the early stages should include taking shelter, changing into warm, dry clothing and drinking plenty of hot fluids – see Chapter 7 for some survival skills. But there is a requirement for urgent medical treatment at all stages of hypothermia and the further the sufferer is allowed to slide, the more critical this is.

First-Aid Kit

Whenever you undertake any activity that could involve injuring yourself, you should always carry a first-aid kit with you to tide yourself over until you can get professional help. If you are training or hiking in the hills, when help can be hours or even days away, this becomes doubly important and a first-aid kit is a vital component of your survival equipment.

All the components of a first-aid kit should be packed in an airtight, waterproof container and secured in your rucksack or sports bag where you can easily get to it in an emergency. If possible, mark the container with a big red cross to indicate its contents to any third party who is helping you.

Avoid carrying items in your first-aid kit that might cause side-effects or strong allergic reactions. Conversely, if you suffer from hay fever, asthma or similar complaints, make sure that you carry your medication with you. Depending on where you are training, you may also wish to carry a sunscreen and some insect repellent.

Bandages

Carry a small selection including a triangular bandage for making slings and some rolled bandages for securing dressings, wrapping bruises and sprains, and so forth.

Plasters and Dressings

Carry a selection of different sizes and shapes for dressing cuts, small burns and minor abrasions. Always leave them in their sterile wrapping until you need to use them.

Surgical Spirit

A small bottle of surgical spirit is useful for cleaning wounds and sterilizing blades, pins and so on.

Petroleum Jelly

Carry a pot of petroleum jelly for use as a preventive against blisters and chafing.

Painkillers

Aspirin, paracetamol, ibuprofen (Nurofen) and similar painkillers are very effective against mild to moderate pain. Make sure that you don't exceed the manufacturer's recommended dosage with these tablets as overdosing can be very dangerous.

Safety Pins

These can be used to secure bandages and also, after sterilization, to empty blisters. Carry several of different sizes.

Water Purification Tablets

If you are in the hills for any length of time, you are likely to exhaust your own water supply. 'Puritabs' will sterilize suspect water, although they generally affect the taste for the worse. Follow the maker's instructions.

Anti-Diarrhoea Tablets

Imodium or a similar brand of tablet can help to relieve attacks of diarrhoea. Diarrhoea can cause acute dehydration and should be taken very seriously, particularly when you are in remote areas.

6 INJURIES

79

YOU DON'T NEED to be a soldier or a mountaineer to enjoy the Great Outdoors, just as you don't need to be an SAS trooper or Commando to get fit. Scrambling through hills and countryside can be immensely enjoyable in its own right, but there is the bonus that it is also very good for you. It helps to get you fit, you breathe clean air and it can ease the stresses and strains that come from the pressure-cooker lives that most of us lead in cities and towns. But whether you want to enjoy the Great Outdoors for its own sake, or you are using it as a training area for an attempt at SAS selection or P-Company and the Commando course, you need to know what you are doing.

Every time the weather closes in, there are news

CHAPTER 7
THE GREAT OUTDOORS

reports of groups of hikers getting lost in remote areas. Often such cases end in tragedy, for even in a comparatively mild climate it is possible to succumb to exposure very quickly. And yet with a little preparation, some forethought and a big dollop of common sense, you can avoid the worst of the pitfalls.

This chapter covers the basic knowledge that you will need before you should even consider going into the hills. It doesn't pretend to be comprehensive, but it does explain the factors that you need to be aware of before you set off. If you are keen to sample life in the Great Outdoors, read this chapter, digest it and start planning. But don't get out there until you are 100 per cent sure that you know what you are doing.

SPECIAL EQUIPMENT

CHAPTER 1 SHOWED you exactly what equipment you need to get started in normal fitness training, up to and including the full Fighting Fit programme. But some people will be going all the way – to SAS selection and, perhaps, beyond. This section deals with the kit that you should consider using for hillwork generally and for SAS selection. It was designed and constructed for use in extreme conditions and you could do a lot worse than take it on your next hiking trip!

Boots

A comfortable pair of boots that fit properly is of the utmost importance to any hiker. It is particularly important on SAS selection, simply because of the enormous distances that you will have to march in them. There are two military-issue types that are worth considering and a number of civilian alternatives.

'Boots, Combat, High'

'Boots, Combat, High'

These are the current standard-issue army boot. If you have a pair that fits properly, are waterproof, still have most of their tread and are thoroughly broken in, you can't go wrong. Unfortunately, this state of affairs is not as common as it should be and a design flaw in older types also meant that they caused Achilles tendonitis in some users. Not bad for the money but you can do a lot better.

'Boots, Jungle, US Pattern'

American jungle boots, as worn in Vietnam, are increasingly popular in the army for a number of reasons: they are lightweight, easy to break in and they have a very deep tread, but the drawbacks are that they are not at all waterproof and don't offer your ankles much support. Worth thinking about in good summer weather only.

'Boots, Jungle, US Pattern'

Danner Boots

Danners, Rockies and other similar designs have only made an impact in the last five years. They are civilian designs which generally use composites of leather and the various new breathable waterproof fabrics (such as Gore-Tex) to produce boots that are dry, very comfortable and require minimal breaking in. The one drawback is their high price which reflects the cost of the materials used in their construction, but if you can afford them, buy them.

> Military surplus outdoor equipment is generally well made, rugged and quite cheap, but don't dismiss purely civilian items. For safety reasons, for example, walkers should wear highly visible, brightly coloured civilian waterproofs in preference to the camouflaged military version.

7 THE GREAT OUTDOORS

Lightweight Walking Boots

Lightweight Walking Boots

These have become very popular as well. In design they are quite similar to a strongly constructed, ankle-high running shoe. While generally they aren't very waterproof, they are very comfortable, particularly over long distances. The most popular brands are Hi-Tec 'Trails' and Karrimor 'KSBs'.

Danner Boots

To improve their waterproof performance, all these boots can be worn with gaiters which will stop some water getting in over their tops.

Rucksacks

You will be issued a rucksack when you turn up for SAS selection or P-Company, but you need to have one to take into the hills anyway. Essentially, the choice is between the old, external-frame pattern and more modern internal-frame designs.

SAS Rucksack

The SAS rucksack is a development of the old A-frame Bergan which the SAS used right through the '40s, '50s and '60s. It consists of an enormous nylon main sack with two side pouches and a rear pouch, together with a map pocket and a zipped compartment in the lid. All of this is attached to a General Service frame (also issued for radios, etc.). The advantages of this rucksack are its colossal carrying capacity and the fact that it rides quite high up on the back, above any belt-kit that you might be wearing. The disadvantages are its awkward shape and the fact that many people find the external frame very uncomfortable.

SAS Rucksack

7 THE GREAT OUTDOORS

SPECIAL EQUIPMENT

Berghaus Crusader

Berghaus Crusader

The Crusader rucksack is a good example of a more modern internal-frame design, and it is also the rucksack that the new army-issue PLCE rucksack is based on. It has a slightly smaller capacity than the SAS rucksack and is longer and narrower in shape; it also has twin side pouches that can be detached to form a day-pack with some additional straps. The longer length means that the bottom of the pack can interfere with belt-kit, but by way of compensation it is provided with a waist-belt which helps to spread the load between the shoulders and the hips.

Which to Choose?

This is purely a matter of personal preference, but for general use an internal-frame design of the kind made by Berghaus, Karrimor, Lowe and others (or even the new army-issue PLCE rucksack) is recommended purely on the grounds of comfort. Most of them have

plenty of pockets and zipped compartments, and they even come in some nice bright colours. You should also choose a rucksack which has a drawstring hood to stop water getting in to the main compartment.

Clothing

Clothing to wear on the hills is a matter of personal taste and comfort, but this must be tempered by an awareness of just how bad conditions can get. Even in temperate climates, hardened SAS men can get caught out and several have died of exposure while training or on operations.

Bear in mind that it is not a good idea to wear military-style clothing in the more remote parts of the world, where you may easily be mistaken for more than an innocent hiker.

Underwear

Choose a pair of underpants that aren't going to chafe your legs under your trousers (boxer shorts tend to do this and the result can be agonizing). Even during the summer, wear a thermal vest or T-shirt of the type which will remain warm when wet (try the Helly-Hansen 'Lifa' brand). The most comfortable socks are the loop-stitch wool/nylon variety – if you wear a pair of these, you won't need oversocks.

Shirts

By far the best outdoor shirt is the cotton loop-stitch Norwegian Army shirt which you can buy in various colours from army surplus and camping stores.

Trousers

The best trousers to wear over long distances in the hills are the lightweight poly-cotton variety which don't retain water and dry fairly quickly. Army 'green light-weights' and jungle combat trousers fit this description if you want to wear military kit. You could also consider wearing 'Ron Hill Tracksters' or similar stretchy nylon track-suit trousers. Do not, however, go hiking in jeans: they soak up water and offer little protection from the cold.

Opposite: Fair weather gear for walking in the hills

SPECIAL EQUIPMENT

Pullovers

Always carry at least one pullover in your rucksack even if you don't wear it. The 'fibre-pile' variety (as made by Helly-Hansen and others) is excellent, as the pile usually retains warmth even when wet. Some members of the Special Boat Service wear a Marks & Spencer lambswool crewneck pullover (in a suitably tactical colour!) in place of a bulky sweater.

Jackets

Most soldiers swear by the 'windproof smock', a lightweight, camouflaged, cotton combat jacket with a hood issued to the SAS and other specialist units but bought and worn by just about everybody. The smock can be made water-resistant to some extent, but its great advantage is that it dries reasonably quickly and has lots of big pockets. It is available in non-military colours from camping stores.

Hats

You should wear a hat to keep the sun off you in the summer and one to keep your head warm in the winter (a motorcyclist's Balaclava or a ski hat are ideal for this).

Waterproofs

A decent set of waterproofs is essential if you are training anywhere at all remote – they can mean the difference between life and death. For training purposes, buy a brightly coloured set because if you do get lost or injured, it will be easier for rescuers to find you. Carry both a jacket and overtrousers.

> You should plan to make the minimum impact on the environment that you are visiting. The SAS trains its soldiers to leave no trace of their passing when they are in remote areas, and to protect the environment everyone should adopt the same principles. This means that you must plan to carry all rubbish with you, avoid damaging fences and walls, avoid using the countryside as a lavatory and avoid disturbing plants and animals. You should not attempt to live off the land unless you really have to, as this causes far more damage than the experience is worth!

7 THE GREAT OUTDOORS

HILLWORK

THERE ARE A number of factors to consider before you set off, all of which can be important to the final outcome of a trip into the hills and whether you get any enjoyment from it. Consider all of these points when you first start planning:

The Aim
If you want to go to the hills to train for SAS selection, then you won't want to take your granny. On the other hand, if you simply want to relax and enjoy yourself for a couple of days in the mountains, she might be an ideal companion. Establish what your aim is and base the rest of your planning on that.

The Area
If you don't have any climbing or scrambling experience, you probably won't have much fun in an area of crags and rocks. Match your choice of area to your experience and that of any companions.

Travelling Companions
Take people with you who have the same aims as you. If you are new to hillwork, try to persuade an old hand to go along with you, and in any event remember that what you achieve will be at the level of the least able member of your group. Ensure that everybody in the group is fit enough and that nobody has any medical problems that are likely to cause difficulties.

Maps
Get sufficient copies of the mapping for the area so that everyone has a full set (and make sure that they can all use them!).

Safety and Emergency
Establish emergency drills and make sure that every member of the group is completely familiar with all of them. If in doubt, consult with the local police or mountain rescue team.

> On at least one of the SAS selection marches, candidates are given a very basic sketch map with which to reach their objectives. This helps prepare them for operations in areas where mapping may be sparse, inaccurate or even non-existent.

Safety Rules

Until you have gained experience of the conditions which you will meet in the hills, there are a number of safety rules that you should always follow. Ignore these at your peril: you will be storing up problems which may only hit you when you are too far from safety to do anything about them. These are the most important:

> 1 Never travel alone. If you do and you get seriously injured, there will be nobody to turn to.
> 2 Always tell somebody sensible, preferably in writing, precisely where you are planning to go and when you plan to finish. Arrange for them to contact a specific police or mountain rescue post if you are late.
> 3 Don't sleep out in the hills until you know exactly what you are doing.
> 4 Always carry an emergency first-aid and survival kit (see the survival section later in this chapter).

Afterwards

When you finish a trip into the hills, it is always worth sitting down (over a beer or two; after all, you've earned it) and discussing what was good and what was bad about it with your travelling companions. Only by doing this will you improve your performance and learn from your mistakes. The first question to ask is whether you managed to achieve your aim. If you did, that's all well and good (though you should think about the factors that helped you and those that were a hindrance), but if you didn't then ask yourself what went wrong. Perhaps your aim was too ambitious or you tried to go too far or too fast – in which case plan to be more realistic next time or work harder on your fitness. If you had an accident or there were medical problems, work out exactly what caused them and seek to avoid them in future. Sensible self-criticism has always been a feature of the British Army's elite units and it is an activity that can be profitably expanded into civilian life. Self-confidence is a fine thing, but don't let it get the better of your common sense.

MAPS

THE ABILITY TO navigate accurately is crucial to any kind of hill-walking, particularly if you want to venture into more remote areas. Anyone who turns up for SAS selection, P-Company or the Commando course who can't read a map is in for a very rude awakening.

The first element in navigation is understanding your map. A map is, quite simply, a graphic representation of the surface of the earth as if seen from above. The best map coverage of Great Britain is provided by the Ordnance Survey in their 1:50,000 Landranger series for which there are 204 component sheets, but there are maps to the same scale for most of the rest of the world which are generally fairly good. All references in this section are to the Ordnance Survey series.

Basic Information

The first thing to look at when you open a map is the basic information printed on the cover or round the edges. This tells you the area covered, when the map was printed (which can be useful because it is possible

that new features, like roads and bridges, have been built), the contour interval, the scale and the grid magnetic angle. You need to pay special attention to the last three.

Scale

The scale on Ordnance Survey Landranger maps is 1:50,000. This means that 2 centimetres of map is equivalent to 1 kilometre of real ground (Ordnance Survey maps are now metric, and therefore in mapwork distances are given in kilometres, not miles). This will help you accurately to judge the distance between two points marked on your map, though this won't be as the crow flies – you must allow for the contours of the ground.

Contour Interval

Contours are light brown lines drawn on the map which link together points of equal height. The contour interval is the distance up or down that each line represents. These can vary between old and new maps but

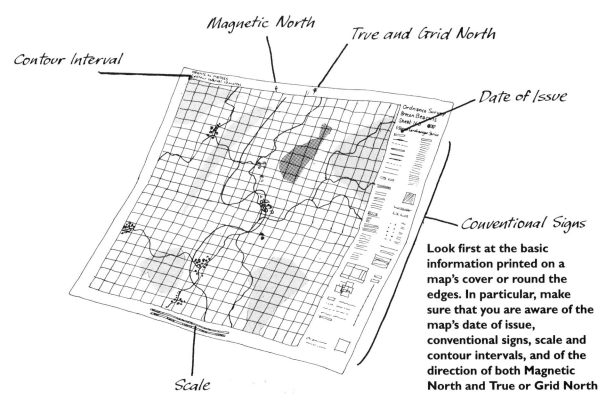

Contour Interval

Magnetic North

True and Grid North

Date of Issue

Conventional Signs

Scale

Look first at the basic information printed on a map's cover or round the edges. In particular, make sure that you are aware of the map's date of issue, conventional signs, scale and contour intervals, and of the direction of both Magnetic North and True or Grid North

it is currently set at 10 metres (just over 32 feet). The closer the contour lines, the steeper the gradient. As you gain more experience with maps, you will build your understanding of how the contour lines show the shape of the ground.

Grid Magnetic Angle

The grid magnetic angle (or GMA) is the variation between the north point indicated by the grid lines on the map and magnetic north, which is where your compass will point. This changes all the time, but you can calculate the current angle by using the information printed on the top of your map.

The rest of the basic information printed around the edge of your map is mainly devoted to an explanation of the 'conventional signs' that represent features on the ground. Thus you find on Ordnance Survey maps that a small circular black blob with a cross on the top represents a church with a spire, while a cross on its own is a church without a spire or a tower. Try to learn as many of these as possible because it will save you time out on the ground.

Grid References

Overlaid on the map is a pattern made up of light blue squares. This is the grid from which, with only a little effort, you can extract a reference which will give your position accurately to within 100 metres. Along the bottom and up the sides of the map are light blue numbers which each correspond to one of the lines of the grid (they are also repeated every 10 lines on the map itself). The grid reference of each square is denoted by the numbers of the two lines which meet in the bottom-left corner and is given as a four-figure group. The first two numbers are of the line which runs vertically (known as 'eastings' because they are numbered from west to east); the second two numbers are from the line that runs horizontally ('northings' because they are numbered from south to north). You can further subdivide the square by imagining ten additional divisions on the easting and northing which give you 100 smaller squares within the main square, each of which represents an area of 100 metres by 100 metres. This is expressed as a six-figure grid by combining the easting and northing together, for example 123 (easting) and 456 (northing) would be given as GR (for Grid Reference) 123456.

Using a Map on Its Own

You can navigate by map alone if you have a good idea of where you are to start with and can understand the conventional signs and the shape of the ground. You need to be in a position where you can see features on the ground like rivers, roads, buildings and hills and relate them to the corresponding symbols on your map (while bearing in mind the scale). This is not an easy trick to master, but you will improve your ability with practice (acquiring the Ordnance Survey sheet of your home area would be a good start).

Protecting Your Map

Finally, it is no use being lost in the hills with a map that has turned into soggy pulp because of the rain, so you need to waterproof it. The best way to do this is with clear fablon – or a similar self-adhesive, transparent, waterproof material – stuck to the front *and* back of your map. Camping stores sell clear plastic map pouches, but you should still waterproof any map that you take out with you.

Establishing a grid reference: subdivide each square on your map's grid by imagining 10 smaller divisions on each side – you can then obtain a highly accurate grid reference. In this case, the church with a steeple is at Grid Reference 007556

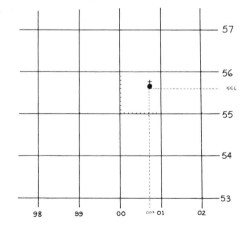

USING A COMPASS

A VERY WIDE range of compasses are available for an equally diverse number of tasks, but the most suitable for general outdoor use are the type made by Silva and Suunto. These are constructed mainly from transparent plastic and feature a baseplate and a rotating dial. Buy one marked in 'mils' rather than degrees, as mils allow you to be more accurate.

Mils

Mils are a more accurate alternative to degrees. There are 6400 mils in a circle as opposed to 360 degrees. Consequently, south is on a bearing of 3200 mils rather than 180 degrees, west is 4800 mils and so forth. With a little experience, mils become second nature.

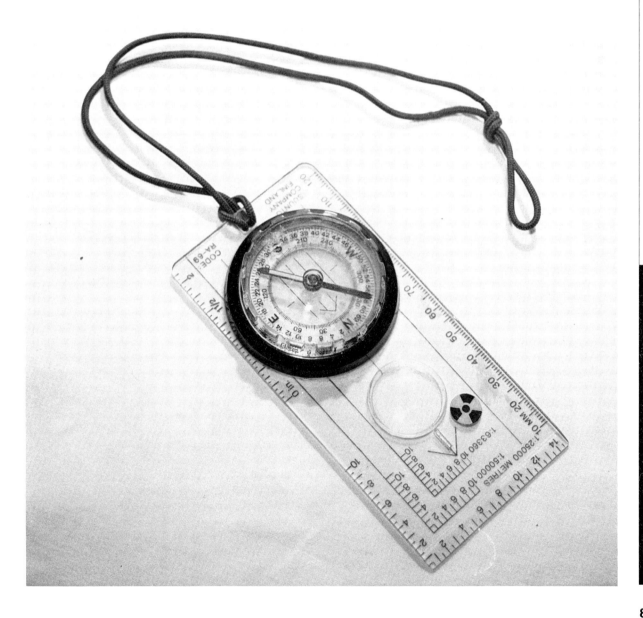

USING A COMPASS

Compass Deviation

The needle on your compass does not point towards 'grid' north (the north indicated by the gridlines on your map); instead it points towards the magnetic north pole. This means that you will need to make a quick, simple calculation when you are converting a bearing shown on your compass to one that you would mark on your map, and vice versa. The formula for this has become a military mantra:

> Grid to Mag, Add; Mag to Grid, Get Rid

This means that when you are converting a 'grid' bearing to a 'magnetic' (mag) bearing, you should *add* the Grid Magnetic Angle (as shown at the top of your map) to the original grid bearing to get the magnetic figure; and when you are converting a mag bearing to a grid bearing, you *subtract* the Grid Magnetic Angle. Easy, isn't it? You should also remember that metallic objects can affect the reading shown by your compass, so don't try taking compass bearings from inside a car, for example.

Setting Your Map

Get out your map and lay it flat on the ground. Line up your compass so that the direction arrow, the N (north) marking and the needle are all pointing in the same direction. Place your compass on top of the map and rotate the map until the compass is pointing north on the map.

> You can use your watch as a basic compass if it has hands. In the northern hemisphere, you should hold the watch horizontal and point the hour hand at the sun. The angle half way between the hour hand and the twelve o'clock marking is the north/south line. In the southern hemisphere, you point the twelve o'clock marking at the sun and the angle half way between that and the hour hand is the north/south line.

Taking a Compass Bearing from Your Map

This involves using your compass as a protractor. All you need to do is place one of the long edges of your compass along the line of the two points that you are taking the bearing between. Position the dial so that the N marking is pointing north on the map and you will be able to read the correct *grid* bearing where the direction arrow meets the dial. If you wanted to walk along this bearing using the compass, you must convert it to a *magnetic* bearing by adding the Grid Magnetic Angle (remember: 'Grid to Mag, Add').

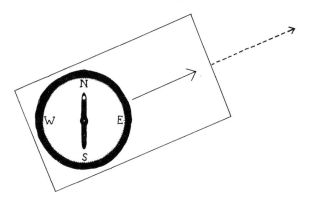

Taking a Bearing
1 Set dial and needle to North.
2 Point arrow (direction of travel) at target.
3 Read off the bearing at the intersection.

Finding Your Position Using Compass and Map

To take a bearing on an object, simply ensure that the compass dial and needle are properly set towards north and then point the direction arrow at your target. This is, of course, a magnetic bearing; convert it to a grid bearing by subtracting the Grid Magnetic Angle ('Mag to Grid, Get Rid'). Now identify the object on your map and use your compass as a protractor to draw on the map, as accurately as you can, the bearing that you have just taken. Do this to at least two more objects and you will find that you have a small triangle where the three lines meet. Your position will be at the approximate centre of this triangle.

CROSS-COUNTRY MOVEMENT

CROSS-COUNTRY MOVEMENT, not surprisingly, is very different from skanking along your local shopping precinct. In the hills your route and speed of travel are almost entirely dictated by features on the ground such as hills, valleys, rivers, streams, bogs, fences, crags and so on. This section covers the various factors which can help and hinder you as you walk through the hills.

Naismith's Rule

Naismith was a Scottish climber in the nineteenth-century who formulated the rule that (translated into metric measurements) an averagely fit person will cover 1 kilometre every 12 minutes, but for each contour line crossed (up or down) you should add a minute to that time. This means that on flat ground you should be able to manage 5 kilometres (approximately 3 miles) per hour.

Hills

The most obvious obstacles to movement are hills and mountains. Even if a hill is directly in between you and your objective, it can frequently be quicker to go round it (contouring) than directly over the top. One of the features of SAS selection is that checkpoints tend to be at or near the tops of hills; if you do have to go to the summit, you should zig-zag up rather than walk in a straight line. Similarly, if you come across a valley (or 're-entrant' as they are called in armyspeak), it may be quicker to skirt round the top of it than go down one side and up the other.

Rivers and Streams

Crossing rivers and streams can be a very risky business, particularly in mountainous areas where they tend to be somewhat faster-flowing. If you can, always find a bridge or ford which you know to be safe; if you can't find one, look for a slower, shallow section which doesn't come above your knees. Do not attempt a river crossing when it is any deeper unless you really have to.

CROSS-COUNTRY MOVEMENT

Bogs

Avoid bogs if you can because they seriously slow you down. When you do cross boggy ground, try to keep to the drier bits (which usually have the most grass and vegetation). You will generally find 'babies' heads' on boggy ground: these are tufts of thick grass on clods of earth which, with care, you can step on to avoid getting your feet too wet. Be careful, however: babies' heads can be treacherous and have led to a lot of twisted ankles and knees.

Crags

Crags and rocky outcrops are best avoided completely unless you are properly kitted out and trained for climbing. Even if this is so, you are unlikely to save much time by attempting to clamber up or down a crag when you could go round it, and you will be much less tired.

Fences

The noble art of fence-crossing is learnt by experience. Use a stile if one is nearby, otherwise chuck your rucksack over and cross next to a sturdy support to avoid damaging the fence. Be sure to check that the fence isn't electrified (I once received a shock to my package crossing an electric fence that left my eyes watering for days!). Deal with drystone walls in the same way, being careful to replace any stones that you dislodge.

Forests

Dense forests slow you down and can often disorientate you. Unless you are sure of your route, skirt round them and pick up your bearing on the other side.

All this should tell you that if there is a path, use it! Paths and roads allow you to travel fast enough to make up all the time that you lose floundering about in the cuds.

THE WEATHER

ONE OF THE most critical factors in hillwork is the weather. Unless you can understand and respond to adverse weather conditions, you may drop yourself so far into it that that you'll never come out. Even in temperate climates the weather can change with surprising speed: what started out as a sunny summer stroll can turn into a nightmare of wind and rain, and the unprepared walker will quickly succumb to exposure.

Weather Forecasts

Everyone likes to knock the weather forecasters, but the truth is that they are usually pretty close to the mark. When you are heading into a remote area, *always* make sure that you are aware of the local weather forecast before you leave. There is a natural tendency to underestimate the severity of conditions, so allow for the fumble factor when you pack your kit and you won't go far wrong. For example, if 'wintry showers' are forecast, pack your blizzard gear.

Weather Patterns

Forecasters make their predictions on the basis of the movement of large masses of air, the measurement of air pressure and air temperature. They combine this with geographical features to assess where it is likely to rain and where it will stay dry. Mountainous regions combine with the wind to force air upwards, causing condensation at high altitudes and thus rain and snow.

Depressions

If the forecasters tell you that there is a depression or trough on the way, expect wind, rain, sleet or snow. Depressions are areas of low pressure which are particularly associated with bad weather. On the seaboard of Western Europe, most weather systems come from the Atlantic Ocean, those from the north generally being somewhat colder than those from the south. Whichever direction a depression comes from, take note, because if you are caught unawares you may be in trouble. A particular problem in the mountains is that depressions bring plenty of cloud with them which can blanket areas of high ground and reduce visibility to a minimum.

Anticyclones

An anticyclone is an area of high pressure normally associated with fine, or at least stable, conditions. In the winter this can mean that it will get extremely cold, particularly at night, but at least it shouldn't rain. A problem for hill walkers caused by high pressure is mist, formed by water vapour being condensed in cold air.

Weather Fronts

Weather fronts are components of depressions, and they are significant in that they are a physical signal of a change in the weather. The most noticeable part of a frontal system is the warm front, which is generally identifiable by wispy cirrus clouds at high altitudes. If you see these when you are in the mountains, take them as a warning that rain (or snow) is on the way with the cold front that follows on behind. You can identify the arrival of a cold front by the appearance of thick, gloomy, nimbostratus clouds.

Following pages:

Altocumulus (A)
Fair weather clouds consisting of smallish, broken up masses with shadows in them. They often appear after stormy weather.

Cumulonimbus (B)
The classic large storm clouds which may develop tops like an anvil. They are an indication that rain (or hail) and strong winds are on the way.

Cirrus (C)
Cirrus clouds with their hooks and sheaves indicate the approach of disturbance and a change in the weather.

Cirrostratus (D)
These have a stringy look to them. If the sky becomes covered with cirrostratus clouds, and particularly if the sky begins to darken above them, rain or snow are on the way.

Nimbostratus (E)
These form a low, gloomy blanket of cloud. They usually mean wet weather (rain or snow) within a few hours, and often the wet is prolonged.

CLOUDS

A

Many of the old wives' tales about weather prediction are true; when bad weather is on the way rheumatic aches and pains increase, curly hair becomes tighter and less manageable, and forest smells become stronger and more distinctive. Learn to look for nature's indicators and you will have a surprisingly accurate method of making short-term forecasts.

B

C

96

D

E

NIGHT NAVIGATION

MOVING AT NIGHT can be dangerous and frightening, particularly in unknown territory. Navigation is often difficult because you cannot make out landmarks in the distance. Nevertheless, there will be times when you have to travel at night and this section gives you some guidelines on how to set about it.

Night Vision

It is never completely dark in open country. After a while – 30 minutes to an hour – your eyes will have become accustomed to the darkness, and you should be able to see a considerable amount (in bright moonlight you will be able to see almost as much as you can during daylight hours). However, if you then look at bright lights you will have to acquire your night vision all over again. The answer to this is to keep one eye closed and shield the other as much as possible from any light source until it has gone. If you have to use a torch, place a red filter over the lens which will help to protect your night vision.

Walking at Night

Aside from the other difficulties, darkness masks the minor hazards that appear underfoot, like ditches, tree roots, rocks, puddles and so forth. The best way to avoid injuring yourself at night is to walk slowly, testing each step before you put all your weight on it. When travelling down steep slopes, use short, shuffling steps and lean backwards as far as you can so that you can sit quickly to avoid a fall. Avoid walking through forests at night, as they will be much darker than surrounding open countryside.

Using Your Compass

You should use your compass in the same way that you would during the daytime, but you will have to move in much shorter 'bounds' because your view of distant objects will be limited. If you are going to have to travel

Finding True North (Northern Hemisphere)

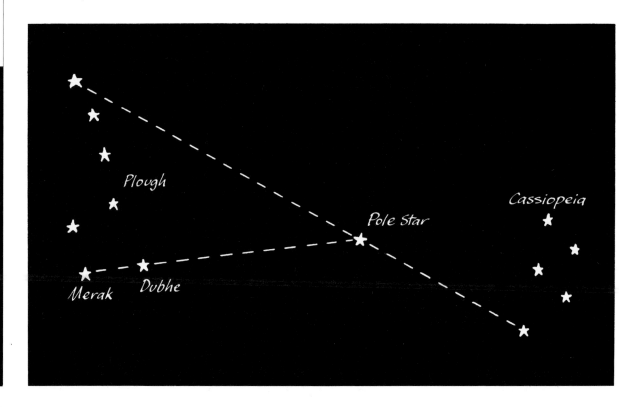

much at night, you ought to have a compass with luminous markings on the dial and you need to be as familiar with the way it looks in the dark as you are during daylight hours.

Astral Navigation

You don't have to be an expert to obtain a good general idea of your direction from the stars. In the northern hemisphere the Pole Star is located almost directly above the North Pole, while in the southern hemisphere the Southern Cross provides a good general indicator for true south.

Finding the Pole Star
The two constellations which help to find the Pole Star are the Plough (or Big Dipper) and Cassiopeia (alias 'The Big W'). Both constellations wheel round the Pole Star and are on opposite sides to it. In the Plough, the stars Merak and Dubhe point directly towards the Pole Star.

Using the Southern Cross
There is no easily recognizable star which marks the South Pole, but the Southern Cross provides a good general indicator. The Southern Cross itself is located on the Milky Way, beneath a large dark patch called the Coal Sack. To find south, you must imagine a line projecting along the cross but four and a half times longer. Drop your imaginary line down to the horizon and that is south.

Finding Directions
Once you have located the direction of the North or South Pole, you should drive two sticks into the ground so that you can sight along them towards the Pole like a rifle sight. The line between them indicates north and south and you can then draw lines to indicate east and west.

Finding True South (Southern Hemisphere)

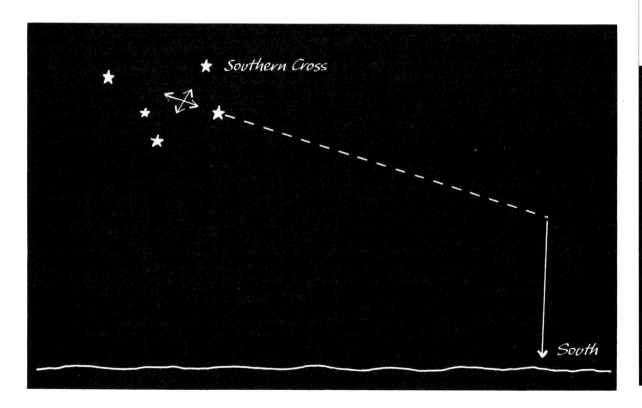

SURVIVAL KIT

DISASTER CAN STRIKE very quickly in the hills and you must ensure that you are carrying the right equipment to help you cope with it. This section is about the survival equipment that you should carry for training or walking in the hills for short periods. If you are undertaking a long expedition, I recommend that you read *The SAS Survival Handbook* by John Wiseman (published by Harvill) which is a comprehensive guide to survival in all conditions.

Knives

For hill walking you will be best served by a folding pocket-knife of the Swiss Army type – though beware of cheap imitations. The largest model, which includes a magnifying glass and other extras, is unnecessary, but your knife should have a good blade, a saw and a small pair of scissors at least. Some camping and army surplus stores sell huge, frightening, Rambo-style survival knives. These are normally just extra weight to carry (and a drastic comment on their owner) unless you are planning to live off the land for extended periods in the most remote places.

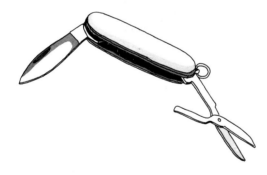

Dry Clothing

Always carry a spare set of dry clothes to change into, and to sleep in, at the end of the day – it's a tremendous confidence-booster. In a survival situation, you may need to change into dry clothes anyway to reduce the risks of exposure.

Poncho

An army-style waterproof poncho or 'basha' is an excellent means of rigging an emergency shelter. Ensure that the one you buy has loops or eyelets to enable you to tie it securely. Also carry some tent pegs to help secure it.

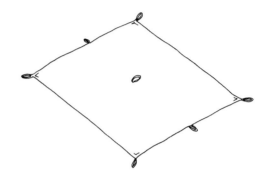

Survival Bag

A survival bag is a large, brightly-coloured, heavy-duty polythene sack that you can climb inside for shelter and warmth when you are stuck in a tight corner or alternatively use as a marker panel to attract the attention of search aircraft. The best sort have a metallicized lining which reflects your body heat back. Don't use them for normal sleeping as you will sweat excessively.

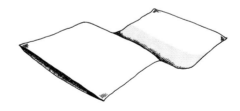

Para Cord

Parachute cord is immensely strong nylon-based string which has a multitude of survival uses. Carry at least 10 metres.

SURVIVAL KIT

Torch

A good quality water-resistant torch, with a red filter to preserve your night vision, is essential. Popular types include the Mini-Maglite and the various brands which can be mounted on a headband, leaving your hands free. Always carry enough spare batteries to last for your entire trip.

Zippo Lighter and Lifeboat Matches

These are the two best methods of lighting fires in high winds. Use the lighter primarily and keep the lifeboat matches (which are simply matches coated in wax) in reserve in case the lighter gets wet. Always carry spare flints for the lighter and make sure that it is filled with fuel before you leave.

Miniflares

Miniflares are an excellent way of attracting the attention of search parties. Don't fool around with them as they can be very dangerous.

Emergency Food

A big bar of chocolate or Kendal mint cake can help keep you going in a survival situation. Don't scoff them unless you really have to – you can save them as a treat for when you finish!

Water Bottle

You can become dehydrated even in wet weather. Always carry a bottle of clean water and some purification tablets. The best water bottles are the army-issue black plastic type (from army surplus stores), and you can get purification tablets from pharmacies and camping stores.

First Aid Kit

As I have suggested in the previous chapter, always carry a selection of bandages, plasters and dressings, a small bottle of surgical spirit, petroleum jelly to prevent chafing and blisters, some painkillers (such as aspirin or paracetamol), safety pins for securing dressings and emptying blisters, water purification tablets (such as Puritabs) and anti-diarrhoea tablets like Imodium. Add a couple of razor blades, which have any number of uses, and some sun cream if there is a danger of burning. Pack the whole lot in a carefully marked, airtight plastic container.

This is only a basic kit. Those going further afield, particularly in the tropics, will need to take many more pills, creams and potions.

SURVIVAL KIT

Survival Extras

You should also strongly consider carrying the following in your kit:

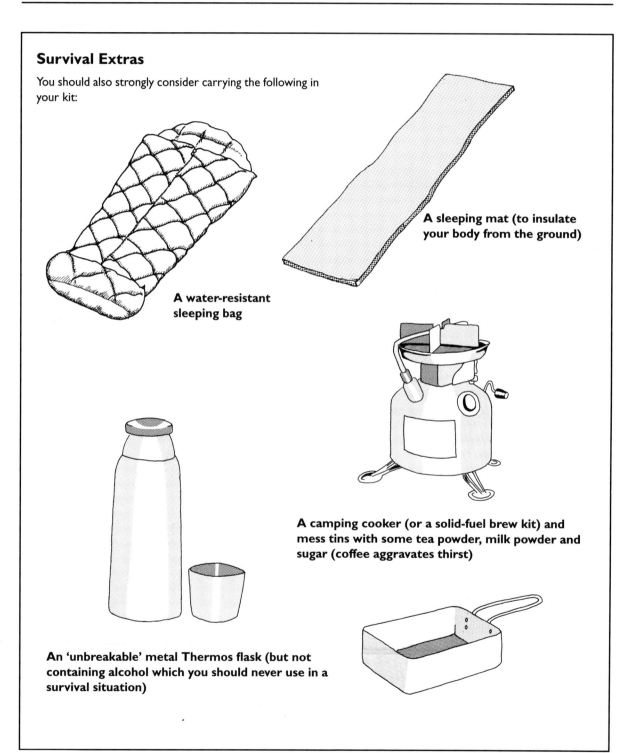

A sleeping mat (to insulate your body from the ground)

A water-resistant sleeping bag

A camping cooker (or a solid-fuel brew kit) and mess tins with some tea powder, milk powder and sugar (coffee aggravates thirst)

An 'unbreakable' metal Thermos flask (but not containing alcohol which you should never use in a survival situation)

SURVIVAL TECHNIQUES

SURVIVAL KITS ARE all very well, but you need to know how to use them or they won't help. Knowledge of the basic survival techniques is essential for anyone walking or training in mountainous areas. If disaster does strike, it may be that positive action will be the only way of saving your own life.

The Survival Priorities

The basic elements of survival are Food, Shelter, Warmth and Water. Their relative importance depends on your particular situation, but if you are simply hill-walking or training in remote areas, shelter and warmth are likely to be the priorities.

Shelter

If the weather or an injury to a member of your party forces you to take shelter, you have the means in your survival kit to make a very efficient one. The first thing to do is find a suitable site. Ideally you want it to be on flat, dry ground with protection from wind and rain. Avoid hill tops, which are exposed to the wind, and valley bottoms which can be wet and always tend to be colder than surrounding areas. Also try to avoid being too close to watercourses and beneath dead trees or branches which may fall on you. Lone trees can attract lightning strikes and are best given a wide berth.

Make your shelter by stretching your poncho between trees or bushes and elevating each end with a stick to make a ridged 'tent'. If there is no vegetation available, you can make guy-lines from para cord and secure them into the ground with your tent pegs, making the ridge by propping a rucksack at either end.

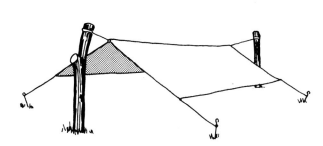

A survival tent made from a poncho and para cord

Where possible, attempt to elevate the centre of the shelter so that water doesn't collect on the surface of it. Use additional ponchos to make groundsheets and wind/waterproofing.

Warmth

Once your shelter is ready, get into it and start preparing your kit. Change into dry gear if your clothes are soaked, or at least wring excess water from your clothing before putting it back on. Make yourself a large hot drink from your flask or brew kit (don't cook inside your shelter as you may set light to it or poison yourself with fumes), or if that isn't possible then eat some of your survival rations and sip some water. If conditions outside are very bad, take off your boots and get into your survival or sleeping bag. It is then a question of waiting for conditions to improve enough for you to move on. When you do move, don't leave any kit behind (you may need it again) and head straight towards the nearest habitation so that you can alert them to your presence and warn off the police and mountain rescuers.

Injury

An injury in the hills presents some difficult choices. The first thing you must do is assess the extent of the injury; a victim who is unable to continue moving should be placed in a dry, warm shelter as soon as possible. If you are in a group of three or more, at least one person *must* stay with the casualty while the others go for help. When you do this, ensure that you know precisely where the casualty is going to be when you return with a rescue party; you should also consider pooling dry, warm gear to keep the casualty comfortable while you get help.

If there are only two of you, the uninjured person will have to decide whether to stay with the casualty or go to get help. In any event you must ensure that the casualty is as comfortable as possible, sheltered, warm and in no further danger. This particularly applies when the victim is in shock, as they will then be very susceptible to hypothermia.

CHAPTER 8
ON
SELECTION

THE SPECIAL AIR SERVICE is, without doubt, the toughest, most professional and highly trained military unit in the world. Feared by their enemies, be they terrorists or conventional troops, they are admired and envied by the special forces of the Western world to whom they are also a big brother, providing advice and support.

In order to reach the ruthless levels of competence that the regiment has achieved, the founders of the SAS long ago realized that the regiment could not be more than the sum of its component parts – the soldiers – and that its operations could only succeed with the highest calibre of men. The instrument that they devised to ensure a consistently high standard of soldier is still used today. Widely acknowledged to be the most searching military course yet devised, it is known simply as 'Selection'.

In their own way, P-Company – the Parachute Regiment's selection course – and the Commando course can be just as demanding as SAS selection. Don't fool yourself that either is a soft option or you will be in for a shock; many SAS regulars began life as paratroopers or commandos. However, these regiments look for slightly different qualities in their recruits, in particular for the stamina, speed and agility required of frontline troops. Training programmes tailored for both courses are included later in this chapter.

The 'Need to Know' Principle

The selection process used by the SAS Training Wing at Stirling Lines in Herefordshire is made up of a number of component parts which combine to give the staff a very clear picture of the capabilities of the aspiring SAS trooper. Many of these are described in off-the-shelf publications about the regiment – but be warned, most descriptions of the selection process have been distorted beyond recognition in the retelling. Part of the value of selection is that the candidate is never quite sure what is going to happen next, and so has to remain alert at all times. This book will get you into peak physical condition for selection, but if it blew the lid off what actually happens on each day of the course, the SAS would only change it. The selection and training of SAS soldiers is, and ought to remain, largely a secret process – but rest assured that the training programme in this chapter has been proved to work!

'Many Are Called; Few Are Chosen'

There is no single physical type of SAS soldier. Once you are in the hills, you will realize that the only thing that is going to get you over them is determination, because no matter how fit you are, it is still going to hurt. The training programme in this chapter will give you the physical strength and endurance to get over the hills, but you have to supply the motivation. At the same time, the SAS require more than simple physical fitness; if you neglect navigation, weapon training, first aid or any of the other basic skills, you might as well not bother to turn up. Only when you are sure that you have what it takes should you volunteer for the SAS selection course.

There are three SAS regiments in Britain. 22 SAS is the regular army unit most recently famous for its successes at the Iranian Embassy, in the Falkland Islands and in Iraq; 21 and 23 SAS – based respectively in the south and west of England, and in the north of England and Scotland – are Territorial Army units open to civilians from all walks of life. It couldn't be more simple to become an operational member of these units – all you have to do is pass selection.

ARE YOU READY FOR IT?

TRAINING FOR SAS selection is no small undertaking. To get the most from your training you will need to devote an enormous amount of both physical effort and time. Before you make the decision to go for it, consider the following factors:

Time

The *Fighting Fit* SAS Selection programme takes up 16 weeks – and assumes that you are fit at the start. Some days you will be taking two separate sets of exercise. Ask yourself honestly if you can afford the time over such a long period. Some units will be able to give volunteers a lot of time off from normal duties to train, but others can't afford that luxury. For security reasons, civilians training for the Territorial Army's SAS units are unable to brief their employers about why they need time for training.

Family

Will your family understand why you are spending so much time away? Take your family circumstances into account before getting too involved in the preparation process. Realistically, you should not be too optimistic about close relationships holding together if you are going to spend all of your free time training.

Money

You may have to spend money on travel to suitable training areas, equipment (like boots and waterproofs) and special foods. Can you afford it?

Motivation

If you can sort out the time, the money and your family life, you are half-way to getting your act together for

ARE YOU READY FOR IT?

an attempt at selection. The other half of the equation is motivation, because you need this for the training as well as the course itself. The big question is: Why do you want to join the SAS? Many very fit candidates will not make it to the end of the course because they are attempting it for the wrong reasons. SAS selection is tough and gruelling because life in the regiment is tough and gruelling. SAS soldiers are paid more than others because they are far more likely to find themselves in uncomfortable, dangerous and life-threatening situations. Candidates for selection are agreeing to play by big boys' rules.

Are You Fit Enough?

The SAS Selection programme given here assumes a reasonable level of cardio-vascular fitness at the start of your training. To have a realistic chance of passing selection, you should be able to run 10 miles in 70 minutes and pass part two of the army's Basic Fitness Test in under 8 minutes 30 seconds when you begin training (see page 124).

Which Selection?

There are two selection courses each year: one during the winter, one during the summer. Advantages of the winter course are that conditions underfoot in the mountains tend to be easier (because grass and vegetation has died back) and there is less risk of dehydration and heat injury. The disadvantages are that the weather conditions can be very severe (several selection candidates have died from exposure during winter courses) and the days are much shorter – making night navigation far more important. Assuming the advantages of the summer course to be the weather conditions and light levels at night, you must decide which will suit your skills best. Generally speaking, there are more applicants for the summer course.

Other Factors

SAS selection is not just about fitness. Regular soldiers attempting the course need to be sharp navigators with a map and compass, their weapon-handling drills should be faultless and they need enough knowledge of first aid to be able to treat the minor injuries, like blisters and cuts, that they will pick up during the course. These can all be practised during your training but if you neglect them, you will have no chance. Finally, and above all, SAS soldiers must be intelligent enough to apply the knowledge that they gain from their training to the problems that will face them during their service with the regiment. Basically, thickies need not apply.

Decision Time

When you're happy that you are ready to start training in earnest, the time has come to throw down the gauntlet. If you're a regular soldier, go to your orderly room and fill out the form; if you're a civilian, telephone your local Territorial SAS squadron – you are about to start the toughest phase of your life.

More than 50 per cent of SAS soldiers come from the Parachute Regiment, but anyone can apply and many do. In recent years a Royal Naval rating has passed selection, a regular SAS squadron has been commanded by an RAF Officer and 22 SAS has been commanded by a Royal Corps of Transport Lieutenant-Colonel.

THE EXTREMES OF ENDURANCE

THE FIRST FOUR weeks of SAS selection is in many ways the ultimate strength-endurance test, and the training programme in this chapter reflects this. Even so, fitness is only one part of it – when you reach the hills, you will find that all kinds of skills and techniques are being tested and you neglect these at your peril. The aim of the training programme described here is to get your endurance and physical strength to a level where you will be able to benefit from the first two weeks of selection in order to peak during the third and fourth weeks and be in top condition for the tests.

Training for Specific Goals

The Fighting Fit programmes in Chapter 5 advocated using sports, like football and rugby, as part of your overall fitness training. For a serious attempt at SAS selection, however, this would be a mistake. The problem is injuries. A rugby or soccer player takes the knocks and plays through them, but imagine the effect of, for example, a bruised knee when you are walking 30 miles across mountainous terrain in the dark carrying a 50-lb rucksack. Treat selection in the same way as an athlete would treat an attempt on a world record and only use exercises that are going to help you achieve your goal. Likewise, you really can't expect to pass if you are getting ratfaced every night or piling down enough smokes to knock out the Marlboro Cowboy.

The Method

The Fighting Fit SAS Selection programme is based on the following exercises, designed to give you the ideal balance between strength and cardio-vascular endurance:

Running
For cardio-vascular endurance and leg strength.

Swimming
For conditioning the upper body and for cardio-vascular endurance without stress on your joints.

Cycling
For cardio-vascular endurance, leg strength and conditioning the abdominals and lower back.

Gym Work
For conditioning the muscles of the chest, shoulders, back, arms and abdomen which are all required to carry a heavily loaded bergan across the mountains.

Bergan Workouts
To develop strength in the upper body and legs by repetitive marching up and down a short hill and to accustom your body to carrying heavy loads.

Hill Training
To accustom you to the actual conditions on selection, and also to increase strength and endurance, sharpen navigation and familiarize you with the terrain that you will be crossing.

Unless you are very lucky you only get two attempts at selection, so make the most of them. Train hard and consistently and don't kid yourself that you're fit enough if you aren't. If something goes wrong while you are on the course, keep trying and push yourself as hard as you can until you're in or you're told to stop. Whatever happens, don't 'voluntarily withdraw' (VW), because you will asked to leave and never come back. Selection is a 'shit or bust' course.

BERGAN WORKOUTS

THE ONE FACTOR that stops most candidates for SAS selection in their tracks is the sheer discomfort of long-distance cross-country marching carrying a heavily loaded bergan. This is irritating for the Training Wing staff as bergan work should form the core of both the physical and psychological conditioning of any candidate on selection – after all, that's how they get tested!

The difference between going for a run and going for a walk carrying a rucksack lies in the effect that it has on your body. When you run, you'll find that you want to stop because you're out of breath and your legs are tired; when you're walking with a bergan, it is your entire body that is straining and your mind is telling you to stop – the difference between those that pass selection and those that don't is whether they can make themselves continue under these circumstances. Any bergan training that you can do before you get out there on selection will help, but if you don't do any, you are very unlikely to pass.

Bergan Training

There are two ways of training with a bergan. You can do short, strength-building sessions, designed to help build up your shoulders, back and thighs during the early stages of your preparation, and you can do much longer endurance workouts, in hill terrain similar to that encountered on selection, which will accustom you to the level of work required for selection itself. This section concentrates on the techniques that you should use for the shorter sessions, but you will find guidance on extended hillwork later in the chapter and in the SAS Selection programme itself. You will need to do plenty of bergan workouts while preparing for P-Company and the Commando course as well as for SAS selection.

Equipment

Boots
Those you're going to wear on selection (see Special Equipment in Chapter 7).

Socks
As for boots.

Clothing
To suit the weather (T-shirt and shorts during the summer, more during the winter).

Water
Get used to carrying, and drinking, water during workouts.

Bergan
The one you are going to use on selection (22 SAS and R Squadron use the new PLCE rucksack; 21 and 23 SAS use the external frame SAS rucksack).

Hill
Very steep and about 200–300 metres long.

Routine

March up the hill and march back down it for the time stated in the 16-week SAS Selection programme. This is boring and painful but absolutely crucial to your subsequent survival on the course. Why not try whistling 'The Grand Old Duke of York' to yourself while you're doing it – at least it will remind you that you're not the first. Push yourself, particularly uphill, as hard as you can, but be sure not to run – carrying weight on your back and wearing boots, this is a sure way to injure yourself. Try wearing a Walkman to take your mind off the workout (don't do this on the course because they'll kick you out).

The Fan Dance

The Fan Dance is the first severe test of fitness that you encounter on SAS selection and it weeds out a considerable number of candidates. It is used here as a training aid and confidence-builder in the 16-week Selection programme because experience shows that candidates who do well on the Fan do well over the next two weeks.

The dance itself takes place in the Brecon Beacons during the first week of selection. It is a forced march between two points via the summit of Pen-y-Fan (hence the nickname), then back again. Get hold of Ordnance Survey sheet 160 in the 1:50,000 Landranger series and look at the bottom right-hand corner. The two points that you march between are the Storey Arms mountain rescue post at grid reference 983204 and the track and road junction at grid reference 049168. Checkpoints that you visit are at the 816-metre summit of Pen-y-Fan at grid reference 012216 and the track junction at grid reference 032206. You are allowed about 4 hours 15 minutes to complete this, but you should aim for 4 hours flat. This will force you to push yourself hard. In training, use the weight suggested in the programme, but in the real thing you will be carrying a weapon and a bergan loaded with 35 lb of gear. Make no mistake: however fit you are, this is going to make you feel terrible afterwards – but don't let that put you off!

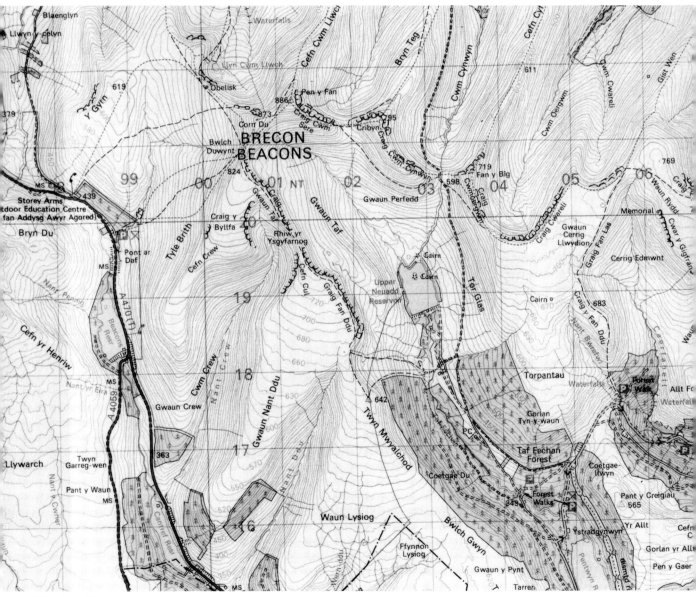

The Fan Dance

TRAINING IN THE MOUNTAINS

THE MAJORITY OF the activities during SAS selection take place in the hills and mountains of Wales and the west of England. The Brecon Beacons are particularly associated with the SAS, but they also use the Cambrians, the Elan Valley, the Malverns and others. If you are planning to do selection, it is essential to familiarize yourself with conditions in these ranges; even if you aren't, they are all fantastic places to go walking and scrambling. Despite the fact that these hills aren't particularly remote, they can still be very dangerous for even the most experienced walker, and they should always be treated with the respect they deserve. The selection programme gives the distances and times you should aim for in the hills, but these two pages contain essential inside information on how to prepare for your training marches.

Clothing

You have to dress to suit the weather and that is largely determined by whether you do the winter or the summer SAS selection course.

Winter

The basic clothing for the winter course should consist of a T-shirt or thermal vest, a Norwegian Army shirt and a windproof smock on your top half with a pair of briefs and lightweight trousers on your legs (you should consider wearing a pair of thigh-length lycra shorts under your trousers to keep your legs warm when your trousers get wet and to prevent chafing). If you wear more than this, you might find yourself getting uncomfortably hot on the more strenuous parts; wear less, and there is an immediate risk of exposure. Additionally, however, you should also carry a good-quality Gore-Tex waterproof jacket which can be worn *underneath* your windproof (to stop damage from your bergan), a fibre-pile jacket or heavy-duty pullover, a warm hat and a pair of warm gloves or mittens.

Summer

Summer weather in the mountains can be just as dangerous as the winter, not least because the variations can be so dramatic, and the summer SAS selection course has accounted for at least one exposure fatality. Consequently, while your basic clothing should be lighter than for the winter, you should always have

Basic clothing for the winter selection course

the warm gear packed in your bergan and ready for use. Probably the most comfortable top to wear on a hot day is the camouflaged jungle shirt which allows you to roll up the sleeves and open the front so that sweat can evaporate (hold in your gut when civilians

TRAINING IN THE MOUNTAINS

What to wear for the SAS's summer selection course

Bergans

Use the same model that you're going to use on selection so that you accustom your body to it; don't cut corners because you will pay the price later.

Contents

The days of carrying rocks or bricks to make up the weight are long gone and the contents of your bergan should reflect the task that faces you. This means that you should carry all of the safety equipment described in Chapter 7, the weatherproof gear just mentioned and anything else that you feel will help you to get over the hills. If for you that means twenty Mars Bars, then carry them!

Water

Always carry at least two full water-bottles with you in the hills, together with a good supply of purification tablets in case you need to drink more than you can carry. Dehydration can be fatal, but if you drink too much water all you do is pass it out again.

Food

If your bergan is underweight, make up the deficiency with food. Sandwiches and chocolate bars are fine if you can handle them, but if they are too much for you then try mixing up Complan or a similar drink with water and some glucose powder. This creates an easily digestible, high-energy meal that you can eat on the move (which is particularly handy on selection itself when there generally isn't time for a white table-cloth luncheon).

A Partner

The most useful piece of kit to take with you into the hills is a partner. A partner is someone to look after you, someone to encourage you and someone to talk to (after eight hours of chatting up sheep, even the raunchiest farmer's boy can get pretty bored), and vice versa.

pass – you don't want to shatter their illusions), with lightweight or jungle trousers to cover your legs. Baldies and skinheads should wear a jungle hat or combat cap to prevent sunburn on their scalps.

THE SAS SELECTION PROGRAMME

DAY	WEEK 1	WEEK 2	WEEK 3	WEEK 4
Monday	Bergan workout – 45 mins, *no weight, no running*	Bergan workout – 45 mins, 15 lb weight, *no running*	Bergan workout – 45 mins, 20 lb weight, *no running*	Run – 1 hour at steady pace, not less than 8 miles
Tuesday	1 Swim – 20 mins 2 Multigym circuit – 30 mins	1 Swim – 20 mins 2 Multigym circuit – 30 mins	1 Swim – 30 mins (45 lengths minimum) 2 Multigym circuit – 40 mins	1 Swim – 30 mins 2 Multigym circuit – 1 hour
Wednesday	Run – 45 mins, 6.5 miles minimum at fastest pace	Run – 1 hour 20 mins, 10 miles minimum at 70 per cent pace	Run – 7 miles with hills at 7.5 minutes per mile maximum	Bike ride – 1 hour
Thursday	Bike ride – 1 hour hard work with hills if possible	Bike ride – 1 hour hard work	Multigym circuit – 1 hour hard work then 20 mins stretching	Bergan workout – 1 hour, 20 lb weight, *no running*
Friday	1 Swim – 20 mins 2 Multigym circuit – 30 mins	1 Swim – 20 mins *straight into* 2 Run – 30 mins at fast pace	Bike ride – 1 hour	Day off – rest and eat
Saturday	Run – 45 mins, 6.5 miles minimum	Multigym circuit – 1 hour 20 mins hard labour	Bergan workout – 1 hour, 20 lb weight, *no running*	Hill training – travel to Highlands, Brecon Beacons, Lake District, Pennines, Dartmoor, etc. Do 2 hours 30 mins of hard marching with 20 lb, *no running*
Sunday	Day off – rest and eat	Day off – rest and eat	Day off – rest and eat	Hill training – 2 hours 30 mins, 20 lb weight, *no running*

The First Month

If you are set on passing SAS selection, by the end of the first month you will have begun to realize how hard you are going to have to work; you will also appreciate the toll that continuously pushing yourself exacts on your body. You will discover that you need to eat more, and rest more, than you have ever done and that your body will not forgive you for late nights and drinking sessions. The value of this is that you are gradually conditioning yourself to the rigours that you will face once you get to Hereford.

THE SAS SELECTION PROGRAMME

DAY	WEEK 5	WEEK 6	WEEK 7	WEEK 8
Monday	1 Swim – 30 mins easy 2 Stretching	1 Swim – 20 mins *then straight into* 2 Run – 30 mins fast	1 Swim – 30 mins easy 2 Stretching	Bergan workout – 1 hour 30 mins, 30 lb weight, *no running*
Tuesday	Run – 1 hour over hills, pushing hard	Bergan workout – 1 hour 30 mins, 20 lb weight, *no running*	Run – 1 hour over hills, 100 per cent effort	1 Swim – 35 mins 2 Multigym circuit – 45 mins
Wednesday	1 Swim – 30 mins 2 Multigym circuit – 40 mins	Multigym circuit – 1 hour	1 Swim – 30 mins 2 Multigym circuit – 40 mins	Run – 1 hour at 100 per cent effort
Thursday	Bergan workout – 1 hour 10 mins, 20 lb, *no running*	Run – 8 miles at 100 per cent effort	Bergan workout, 1 hour, 25 lb weight, *no running but as fast as possible*	Bike ride – 1 hour 15 mins, steady pace
Friday	1 Swim – 40 mins 2 Multigym circuit – 45 mins	Day off – rest and eat	1 Swim – 20 mins *then straight into* 2 Bike ride – 50 mins	Day off – rest and eat
Saturday	Bike ride – 1 hour plus, pushing hard	Hill training – 2 hours 30 mins to 3 hours, 25 lb weight, *no running*	Run – 1 hour 20 mins, steady pace	Hill training – 3 hours to 3 hours 30 mins, 30 lb weight, *no running*
Sunday	Day off – rest and eat	Hill training – 2 hours 30 mins to 3 hours, 25 lb weight, *no running*	Day off – rest and eat	Hill training – 3 hours to 3 hours 30 mins, 30 lb weight, *no running*

The Second Month

As you become accustomed to the workload of training hard, you should start thinking about working on other skills. Find an ace navigator and a good medic and pump them for the skills and techniques that you will need; organize some extra training so that you are completely familiar with every weapon you are likely to meet – remember, neglect your skills and you won't pass.

THE SAS SELECTION PROGRAMME

DAY	WEEK 9	WEEK 10	WEEK 11	WEEK 12
Monday	1 Swim – 30 mins easy 2 Stretching	Run – 1 hour at 100 per cent effort over hills	1 Swim – 30 mins easy 2 Stretching	Bergan workout – 1 hour 30 mins, 35 lb weight, 'rifle', *no running*
Tuesday	Run – 1 hour 20 mins, steady pace	1 Swim – 30 mins 2 Gym – 45 mins	Run – 1 hour 20 mins, steady pace	1 Swim – 45 mins 2 Gym – 1 hour plus
Wednesday	1 Swim – 30 mins *then straight into* 2 Bike ride – 50 mins	Bergan workout – 1 hour 30 mins, 30 lb weight, *no running*	1 Swim – 40 mins 2 Gym – 1 hour	Run – 8.5 miles at best effort pace over hilly route
Thursday	Bergan workout – 1 hour 30 mins, 30 lb weight, *no running*	Bike ride – 1 hour plus, 100 per cent effort over hills	Bergan workout – 1 hour 30 mins to 2 hours, 35 lb weight, *no running*	1 Swim – 45 mins 2 Multigym circuit – 1 hour
Friday	1 Multigym circuit – 1 hour 10 mins 2 Stretching – 20 mins	Day off – rest and eat	1 Swim – 45 mins 2 Multigym circuit – 1 hour	Bergan workout – 1 hour 30 mins plus, 35 lb weight, 'rifle', *no running*
Saturday	Bergan workout – 1 hour 30 mins, 30 lb weight, *no running*	Hill training – 4 hours, 35 lb weight at minimum of 3 miles per hour	Run – 1 hour at 100 per cent effort over hills	Day off – rest and eat
Sunday	Day off – rest and eat	Hill training – 2 hours 30 mins, 35 lb weight at minimum of 3 miles per hour	Day off – rest and eat	Run – 1 hour at 100 per cent effort over hills

The Third Month

In the third month of your preparation you should be consolidating the fitness that you will have built up and honing your military skills prior to moving to the hills for familiarization. Use this month to assess the various aspects of your fitness and work on any that may be deficient – you may not have time later.

The Fourth Month

In the final month of preparation you must get into the hills and get to know the terrain that you will be working in. Use this opportunity to make sure that your equipment is in good order, your map-reading is up to scratch and your motivation is sufficient. In the last week before you start the course it is essential that you rest – it's too late to worry about being fit enough and it is better that your body has the chance to recover from any injuries that you might have picked up in training.

THE SAS SELECTION PROGRAMME

DAY	WEEK 13	WEEK 14	WEEK 15	WEEK 16
Monday	A.M.: Swim – 40 mins P.M.: Run – 8 miles, 7 mins per mile, hilly route	Fan Dance – no more than 4 hours 30 mins, 30 lb weight	Hill training – 7 hours, 35 lb weight, no slower than 3 m.p.h., Brecon Beacons area	Rest
Tuesday	A.M.: Swim – 30 mins P.M.: Gym – 1 hour	A.M.: Swim – 35 mins P.M.: Hill training – 3 hours, 35 lb weight, Brecon Beacons area	A.M.: Swim – 20 mins easy P.M.: Run – 8 miles, hilly course	Run – 30 mins easy, stretch for 20 mins
Wednesday	A.M.: Stretching – 25 mins P.M.: Bergan workout – 1 hour 30 mins, 30 lb weight, 'rifle', *no running*	A.M.: Swim – 30 mins easy P.M.: Hill training – 3–4 hours, 35 lb weight, Black Mountain area	Hill training – 3 hours 30 mins, 85 lb weight (load carry familiarization)	Rest
Thursday	A.M.: Swim – 40 mins P.M.: Bike ride – 1 hour 30 mins at 100 per cent effort	A.M.: Stretching – 25 mins P.M.: Hill training – 3 hours, 35 lb weight, Brecon Beacons area	Hill training – 4 hours, 35 lb weight, fast pace, Elan Valley area	Swim – 30 mins easy, stretch for 20 mins
Friday	A.M.: Stretching – 25 mins P.M.: Run – 1 hour 10 mins over hills	A.M.: Hill training – 4 hours, 35 lb weight, Elan Valley area P.M.: Go home, rest and eat!	A.M.: Fan Dance, 35 lb weight, Maximum time 4 hours 15 mins, gently jog down hills P.M.: Go home, rest and eat	Rest
Saturday	A.M.: Swim – 40 mins (intervals) P.M.: Bergan workout – 2 hours, 35 lb, 'rifle', *no running*	A.M.: Rest P.M.: Run – 1 hour 10 mins, easy pace	Rest	Run – 30 mins easy
Sunday	Day off – travel to Brecon area	A.M.: Rest P.M.: Travel to Brecon	Rest	Report to: Training Wing, 22 SAS, Stirling Lines, Hereford. No more rest!

8 ON SELECTION

P-COMPANY

THE MAROON BERETS of Britain's elite airborne forces are known, and copied, throughout the world as a symbol of military excellence. The 'Maroon Machine' is earned by undergoing P-Company – the pre-parachute selection course.

P-Company itself is an intense experience, designed to test the strength, endurance, will-power and aggression of all volunteers for airborne forces before they are allowed to go forward and be trained as parachutists. It lasts for three weeks and is based at the Airborne Forces Depot in Aldershot and in the Brecon Beacons in Wales. It is a hard course, as tough in some respects as SAS selection, but the emphasis is different. To be successful, a P-Company volunteer needs particularly to train for speed, for upper-body strength and in the curious art of 'tabbing'; there is also the ordeal of 'milling' to go through.

Speedwork

Speedwork must form part of your training programme right from the start. This will develop the power that you need to carry you up and down the seemingly endless 'hill repetitions' that form part of the first two weeks. Intervals, fartlek and simple fast runs will all help you to achieve this.

Upper Body Strength

Most elements of P-Company involve carrying a heavily laden bergan at high speed. The Fighting Fit P-Company programme emphasizes weight and circuit training to help you develop strength in your shoulders, back, chest and abdomen to cope with this.

Tabbing

Tabbing is the fast marching technique that the Paras have developed as an efficient (though knackering) method of getting themselves and their kit into battle. On a tab you must try to average a mile every 10 minutes without running; the technique requires you to push forward strongly with your hips and thighs and swing your arms in an exaggerated manner in order to build a strong forward momentum.

Milling

The longest minute of your life, milling is the P-Company test of aggression. You are given a pair of boxing gloves and an opponent of roughly the same height. The next minute is spent trying to punch each other's heads clean off. You lose marks for turning away or trying to defend yourself. Sounds nasty? It is.

Equipment

You are normally only allowed to wear standard-issue equipment on P-Company, so there is no point in buying any fancy gear. What you must do is ensure that your kit is in excellent condition, clean and serviceable. Boots, particularly, need to be well broken in and comfortable with enough tread to grip on the often slippery assault and confidence courses. You could do worse than obtain a few extra pairs of lightweight trousers and PT vests as your gear will become sweaty and horrible very quickly.

Are You Ready For It?

Don't start training for P-Company until you can run the army's Basic Fitness Test (see page 124) in under 9 minutes 30 seconds and march 10 miles carrying a 30-lb rucksack in under two hours. Servicemen should consider doing one of the 'pre-para' courses run by units of 5 Airborne Brigade which are designed to help potential paratroopers prepare.

THE P-COMPANY PROGRAMME

DAY	WEEK 1	WEEK 2	WEEK 3	WEEK 4
Monday	Run – 45 mins, steady pace	1 Swim – 30 mins 2 Interval workout – 8 × 100 metres	1 Multigym circuit – 45 mins 2 Run – 30 mins easy	1 Swim – 30 mins 2 Multigym circuit – 45 mins
Tuesday	1 Multigym circuit – 30 mins 2 Run – 30 mins easy	Multigym circuit – 30 mins	Interval training – 8 × 200 metres	Interval training – 6 × 400 metres
Wednesday	Interval workout – 8 × 100 metre sprints	Run – 45 mins steady pace	1 Swim – 30 mins 2 Multigym circuit – 30 mins	Run – 45 mins steady
Thursday	1 Swim – 30 mins 2 Run – 30 mins easy	Bergan workout – 30 mins, 15 lb weight, *no running*	Bergan workout – 45 mins, 20 lb weight, *no running*	Bergan workout – 1 hour, 20 lb weight, *no running*
Friday	Bergan workout – 30 mins, 15 lb weight, *no running*	1 Swim – 30 mins 2 Run – 30 mins, fartlek	Run – 45 mins steady	1 Swim – 30 mins 2 Multigym circuit – 45 mins
Saturday	Day Off	Day Off	Day Off	Day Off
Sunday	Run – 1 hour steady	Swim – 45 mins	Run – 45 mins, fartlek	Run – 1 hour steady

THE P-COMPANY PROGRAMME

DAY	WEEK 5	WEEK 6	WEEK 7	WEEK 8
Monday	Tab – I hour, 25 lb weight, *no running*	1 Swim – 30 mins 2 Multigym circuit – 45 mins	Run – 45 mins, fartlek	1 Swim – 30 mins 2 Multigym circuit – I hour
Tuesday	Run – 45 mins, fartlek	Interval training – 8 × 400 metres	1 Swim – 30 mins 2 Tab – 45 mins, 30 lb weight, *no running*	Interval training – 8 × 800 metres
Wednesday	1 Swim – 30 mins 2 Multigym circuit – 45 mins	Tab – I hour, 30 lb weight, *no running*	1 Swim – 30 mins 2 Run – 30 mins steady	Tab – I hour 30 mins, 35 lb weight, *no running*
Thursday	Interval training – 6 × 400 metres	1 Swim – 30 mins 2 Run – 30 mins fast	Bergan workout – I hour, 30 lb weight, *no running*	Easy run – 30 mins
Friday	Run – 45 mins steady	Multigym circuit – I hour	interval training – 8 × 800 metres	Swim – 45 mins
Saturday	Day Off	Day Off	Day Off	Day Off
Sunday	Bergan workout – 45 mins, 25 lb weight, *no running*	Bergan workout – 45 mins, 30 lb weight, *no running*	Tab – I hour I5 mins, 35 lb weight, *no running*	Move to Aldershot for Pre-Para or P-Company

Many of the tests used during P-Company originated in the training for the airborne landing at Arnhem during the Second World War. In that operation, the Paras had to jump on to a drop zone (DZ) outside the town before quickly moving, with all their kit, to seize their objectives around the Arnhem Bridge. This is directly simulated by the P-Company 10-mile march at the start of test week.

THE COMMANDO COURSE

3 COMMANDO BRIGADE are Britain's amphibious warfare specialists. They are mainly drawn from the Royal Marines, who are now virtually all commando-trained, but there are a number of personnel attached to the Brigade from both the Army and the Royal Navy. The Commando course, held at the Commando Training Centre at Lympstone in Devon, earns successful volunteers the right to wear the coveted green beret that has been a symbol of these elite amphibious raiders since the Second World War. The course itself tests a combination of strength and endurance, but unlike P-Company there is also a great deal of instruction and testing in basic commando tactics. Passing the Commando course also earns, for Marines, the right to undergo parachute training without having to pass P-Company, and in consequence about 10 per cent of Royal Marines are also airborne qualified.

The Commandos maintain a much lower profile than the Paras, but this doesn't mean that they are any less hard. Some of the highest in the land have discovered that (as they say in Lympstone), 'You can turn a frog into a prince but you can't turn a prince into a marine'.

Special Features

Two of the most noticeable aspects of the Commando course are the part played by upper-body strength and the requirement for general physical agility. You will undoubtedly do a lot of rope climbing and assault courses, and your preparation should include instruction in these techniques from a qualified instructor.

You must also ensure that your general military skills are up to scratch – that you can easily pass the training tests (TOET) with the rifle, for example, and that your navigational ability is sound.

Are You Ready For It?

The 'passing in' standards for the Commando course require that you can do:

THE PASS IN
50 sit-ups in two minutes
5 pull-ups using an overarm grasp, raising your chest to the bar
Pass the Basic Fitness Test (wearing boots)
Jump into a pool from a high board
Swim 100 metres freestyle
Tread water for two minutes
Pass the Combat Fitness Test
Pass the TOET (rifle training test)

If you have any difficulty with these you won't make it, so aim at the start of your training to be able to conquer them all and then build on that solid base.

The rifle TOET (test of elementary training) at the start of the Commando course is a requirement because of the tactical aspect of much of the training. The TOET requires that a soldier can, safely, clear a rifle; strip and reassemble it; perform the load, unload and make safe drills and, finally, fill a magazine against the clock. More than two errors of drill or any safety errors and the soldier fails.

THE COMMANDO PROGRAMME

DAY	WEEK 1	WEEK 2	WEEK 3	WEEK 4
Monday	1 Swim – 30 mins 2 Run – 45 mins steady	1 Swim – 30 mins 2 Run – 45 mins steady	1 Swim – 30 mins 2 Run – 30 mins fast	1 Swim – 30 mins 2 Run – 45 mins steady
Tuesday	1 Swim – 30 mins 2 Multigym circuit – 30 mins	1 Swim – 30 mins 2 Multigym circuit – 30 mins	1 Swim – 30 mins 2 Multigym circuit – 45 mins	1 Swim – 30 mins 2 Multigym circuit – 45 mins
Wednesday	1 Swim – 30 mins 2 Assault course/rope training	1 Swim – 30 mins 2 Run – 45 mins, fartlek	1 Swim – 30 mins 2 Assault course/rope training	1 Swim – 30 mins 2 Run – 1 hour, fartlek
Thursday	1 Swim – 30 mins 2 Multigym circuit – 30 mins	1 Swim – 30 mins 2 Multigym circuit – 45 mins	1 Swim – 30 mins 2 Multigym circuit – 45 mins	1 Swim – 30 mins 2 Multigym circuit – 45 mins
Friday	1 Swim – 30 mins 2 Interval training – 8 × 100 metres	1 Swim – 45 mins 2 Interval training – 6 × 200 metres	1 Swim – 30 mins 2 Interval training – 8 × 200 metres	1 Swim – 30 mins 2 Interval training – 10 × 200 metres
Saturday	Day Off	Day Off	Day Off	Day Off
Sunday	Run – 1 hour, fartlek	Run – 1 hour, fartlek	Run – 1 hour, fartlek	Run – 1 hour, fartlek

THE COMMANDO PROGRAMME

DAY	WEEK 5	WEEK 6	WEEK 7	WEEK 8
Monday	1 Swim – 30 mins 2 Run – 45 mins steady	1 Swim – 30 mins 2 Bergan workout – 45 mins, 20 lb weight, *no running*	1 Swim – 30 mins 2 Bergan workout – 45 mins, 20 lb weight, *no running*	1 Swim – 30 mins 2 Bergan workout – 1 hour, 20 lb weight, *no running*
Tuesday	1 Swim – 30 mins 2 Multigym circuit – 1 hour	1 Swim – 30 mins 2 Multigym circuit – 1 hour	1 Swim – 30 mins 2 Multigym circuit – 1 hour	1 Swim – 30 mins 2 Multigym circuit – 1 hour
Wednesday	1 Swim – 30 mins 2 Assault course/rope training	1 Swim – 30 mins 2 Run – 1 hour steady	1 Swim – 30 mins 2 Run – 1 hour steady	1 Swim – 30 mins 2 Assault course/rope training
Thursday	1 Swim – 30 mins 2 Run – 45 mins, fartlek	1 Swim – 30 mins 2 Run – 1 hour steady	1 Swim – 30 mins 2 Run – 45 mins, fartlek	Swim – 30 mins
Friday	1 Swim – 30 mins 2 Interval training – 4 × 400 metres	1 Swim – 30 mins 2 Interval training – 6 × 400 metres	1 Swim – 30 mins 2 Interval training – 4 × 800 metres	Run – 30 mins easy
Saturday	Day Off	Day Off	Day Off	Day Off
Sunday	Run – 1 hour, fartlek	Run – 1 hour, fartlek	Run – 1 hour, fartlek	Report to CTCRM

The final test of the first phase of SAS selection is 'endurance', a 40-mile (64 km) march over the Black Mountains and Brecon Beacons carrying a weapon, webbing and a bergan (which must weigh 55 lb/25 kg). Depending on the weather, this march must be completed in around 20 hours. The record stands at under 13 hours, but despite this extraordinary feat the record-holder failed the course.

MEASURING UP

YOU NOW KNOW how to measure your cardio-vascular fitness using the Step Test and the Resting Heart Rate method from Chapter 1, but how do the army test fitness? How would you measure up against a Para, a Commando or an SAS trooper?

The answer lies in two tests that are common to all the units of the British Army, from the Catering Corps to the SAS: the Basic Fitness Test and the Combat Fitness Test.

The Basic Fitness Test

The Basic Fitness Test (BFT) is a simple measure of an individual soldier's ability to run a set distance within a set time limit. It is mandatory for every soldier in the army to run it at least once every six months. Failure can be the start of a slippery slope towards medical downgrading and, eventually, discharge. However, the BFT isn't terribly difficult to pass, though for some it does become a major psychological hurdle and many soldiers who don't take fitness as seriously as they should come to dread its arrival.

The BFT consists of two parts, both run over a 1.5 mile course. Part one is a squadded run/walk, normally done in a group of at least ten men (and sometimes 200 or more) as a warm-up. The squad has 15 minutes to cover the course and alternates between normal 'quick marching' – a fast-paced walk – and 'doubling' at a gentle jog, all of which is done 'in step'. Everybody in the squad should be able to keep up with the pace; if they can't, they have really serious fitness problems.

Part two is another 1.5 miles, often back over the same course, run as an individual best effort. There is no rest between the two parts.

Dress for the BFT normally consists of a PT vest or T-shirt, a pair of green lightweight trousers and training shoes. Until about five years ago the test was done in boots, but it was found that this led to a lot of injuries to the lower leg and the practice was abandoned. The time limit for part two is 10 minutes 30 seconds for all personnel under 30 years old with an increase of 30 seconds for each 5 years thereafter.

Broadly speaking, soldiers who take more than 10 minutes to complete part two need to work on their fitness; those between 9 and 10 minutes are about average; under 9 minutes is good and under 8 is outstanding. It would be unusual to find Paras, Commandos or SAS troopers who took longer than 9 minutes 30 seconds.

The Combat Fitness Test

The Combat Fitness Test (CFT) is normally taken once every year. It is an 8-mile march in full kit carrying a weapon and a helmet and is designed, to some extent at least, to simulate combat conditions. As such, it is difficult to simulate for civilians (and there is little point, anyway), but it is normally the first test encountered on SAS selection.

The CFT is done entirely as a squad – anyone who drops out is scooped up by the 'jack-wagon' that follows on behind – and is normally partly on roads, partly cross-country. Everybody must wear a combat jacket, combat trousers and boots, and they carry 35 lb of personal webbing as well as their helmet and weapon.

A fit squad should be able to do the entire test at a fast walking pace and still get in within the cut-off time of 1 hour and 50 minutes, but a less fit group will find that they have to run on some stretches. Perversely, bigger, perhaps slightly overweight soldiers often find the test easier than the more lightly built because they are better able to deal with the extra weight that they are carrying. Even so, it is not a test that any reasonably fit soldier should have many problems with, provided the squad moves at a sensible pace and doesn't bust a gut trying to set a new world record.

STAY WITH IT

AFTER A FEW WEEKS of taking exercise and eating well, you'll feel great and the statistics are all there to prove it. People who exercise regularly, for example, perform significantly better on measures of reasoning, working memory, reaction time and vocabulary than those who take little or no exercise. It has also been found that exercise alone is as effective as psychotherapy for moderate depression.

And as exercise reduces your risk of premature death by more than half, there are plenty of reasons to start. Even so, you must still keep a sense of proportion. Exercise and a good diet are very beneficial to your sense of well being, but you should not let them come to dominate your life. There will be days when you don't have enough time to take exercise, or when the only food you can get is a burger or two.

If you have managed to discipline yourself to take exercise and eat properly, then you will have developed the mental toughness to accept the occasional setback. Fight back and promise yourself that you are going to overcome the odds. Next time a big marathon is run, watch for the wheelchair athletes as they hurtle round the course and think of the obstacles that they have had to overcome just to compete. I said at the start of this book that it would make you fit and it will, but I never said it was going to be easy!

PICTURE CREDITS

The photographs in this book are reproduced by courtesy of the following: i–ii, Landscape Only; 8–9, Bud Symes Allsport; 20, Bud Symes, Allsport; 33, Allsport; 35, Ancil Nance, Allsport; 37, Simon Bruty, Allsport; 39, Howard Boylan, Allsport; 43, Allsport; 45, Tony Craddock, Science Photo Library; 59, Adam Hart-Davis, Science Photo Library; 60–1, Allsport; 65, Bernard Asset, Allsport; 80–1, Landscape Only; 92–3, Jeff Tucker, Landscape Only; 95, Dr B. Booth, Geo-Science Features Picture Library; 96, Dr B. Booth, GeoScience Features Picture Library; 97, GeoScience Features Picture Library; 104–5, Jeff Tucker, Land-scape Only; 111, Ordnance Survey Landranger sheet 160, © Crown Copyright; 125, RM 45 Commando, Falklands, 1982, Peter Newark's Historical Pictures. All other illustrations are by the author. The publishers acknowledge the rights of the copyright-holders in the illustrations throughout this book.

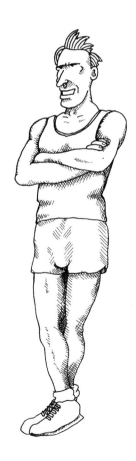

INDEX

INDEX

INDEX